Workshop Models for Family Life Education

Workplace Stress

Nine One-Hour Workshops

Steven B. Zwickel

Families International, Inc.
Milwaukee, Wisconsin

Copyright © 1994
Families International, Inc.
11700 West Lake Park Drive
Milwaukee, Wisconsin 53224

All rights reserved. None of the content of this publication may be reproduced, stored in a retrieval system, or transmitted in any form or by any means (electronic, mechanical, photocopying, recording, or otherwise) without the prior written permission of the publisher.

Library of Congress Cataloging-in-Publication Data

Zwickel, Steven B.
    Workplace Stress : nine one-hour workshops / Steven B. Zwickel.
       p.   cm. — (Workshop models for family life education)
    Includes bibliographical references.
    ISBN 0-87304-252-2
    1. Job stress. I. Title. II. Series.
HF5548.85.Z94   1994
158.7—dc20   94-10230

Printed in the United States

Contents

About the Author 4
Introduction 5

Workshop 1
➤ Introduction to Stress 7

Workshop 2
➤ Dealing with Job Stress 35

Workshop 3
➤ Understanding Anger 61

Workshop 4
➤ Anger in the Workplace 77

Workshop 5
➤ Making the Most of Your Time 99

Workshop 6
➤ Protecting Your Time 119

Workshop 7
➤ Why People Burn Out 137

Workshop 8
➤ Preventing and Treating Burnout 155

Workshop 9
➤ Competition and Cooperation 173

About the Author

Steven B. Zwickel, JD, ACSW, has been an adult education instructor since 1979 and is currently an instructor in the Technical Communications Program, College of Engineering, University of Wisconsin–Madison. He has developed many popular classes, including *Dealing with the Anger in Your Life, Introduction to Stress Management, Cooperative Conflict Resolution, Ethics & Values Clarification, Time Management, Beating Burnout, Building Healthy Relationships, Love & Loving, Launching Your Personal Service Business, Leadership Skill Building, Parenting Children of Divorce,* and *Understanding Stepfamilies.* Over the years, he has run a dispute-resolution program, served as a rural county social worker, and been a family day-care provider. He is the author of *Anger,* another book in the Workshop Models for Family Life Education series.

Zwickel did his undergraduate work at Harpur College. He has a law degree and received a graduate degree in social work from the University of Wisconsin–Madison.

Introduction

Work, it has been said, gives meaning to our lives. We work not only to survive economically, but to obtain intangible rewards such as identity, sense of purpose, and self-esteem.

For our ancestors, work meant scrabbling to harvest enough food to stay alive. The social welfare system developed in response to the Great Depression of the 1930s was designed to protect citizens from losing this struggle for survival. For the first time in our history, people no longer were afraid of starving to death if they didn't have a job. One result of this great economic "safety net" was that people began to look at their jobs as a means of self-fulfillment.

Our expectations of the work world have changed. Although money is still the primary reason we work, other factors such as fame, recognition, power, and status influence our work choices. Some people see their jobs as a way to fulfill important social obligations by helping others and contributing to society. Doing a job well can be a source of personal satisfaction.

The workplace itself has changed greatly in the past 25 years. Thousands of jobs in agriculture and manufacturing have disappeared as our economy has become more service oriented. The new, highly competitive "service economy" relies heavily on the use of computers, resulting in a greater emphasis on speed and productivity.

The environment reflects larger changes that have occurred in society and in the economy. Today, more women work outside the home than ever before; many of these women hold jobs traditionally held by men. Increasingly, women and minority persons are working side by side with white males and competing with them for jobs and promotions.

Our economy remains unpredictable. In the past 15 years, unemployment and inflation have risen and fallen in cycles. Mergers, takeovers, bankruptcies, and layoffs have become commonplace. Widespread access to credit has changed the way we think about savings and debt.

For all of these reasons, the workplace has become a major source of *stress* in people's lives. This book contains a series of short workshops on stress and stress-related topics that can be offered individually or as part of a series built around the theme of stress in the workplace. Each session is about an hour and a half long.

The first workshop introduces various definitions of *stress*, and the second discusses *stressors* in the workplace. The next two workshops focus on *anger* in the workplace, helping participants understand what anger is, how it affects them, and what can be done about it. Another important source of job stress is covered in the two workshops on *time management*; the results of failing to cope with stress are dealt with in the two workshops on *burnout*. The last workshop covers *competition*—another source of job stress. Each workshop includes a selection of handout materials that the instructor can duplicate and distribute to participants. Also, a convenient teaching outline has been provided for each workshop.

Workshop 1
➤ Introduction to Stress

Learning Objectives
- ➤ To provide participants with a better sense of what professionals mean when they talk about stress.
- ➤ To demonstrate how stress derives from various sources.
- ➤ To help participants understand how stress may affect them.

Introduction
A lot of attention has been focused on the effects of stress on our lives. This mini-workshop introduces participants to modern theories about stress and how it affects us.

Handouts
- ➤ Workshop Outline
- ➤ Why Do You Need This Workshop?
- ➤ What Is a Stress Response?
- ➤ Signs of Stress
- ➤ What Does Stress Do to You?
- ➤ Sources of Stress
- ➤ Stress Resources
- ➤ Ways to Reduce the Effects of Stress
- ➤ Evaluation Form

Why a Workshop on Stress?
Distribute the "Workshop Outline" and "Why Do You Need This Workshop?" handouts. Ask participants to fill in as much of "Why Do You Need

Workplace Stress

This Workshop?" as they can. This warm-up exercise helps participants begin thinking about the stress in their lives by asking them to analyze sources of stress, feelings of stress, and existing resources for coping with stress. The question "What was the most stressful thing that ever happened to you?" should be optional, in that the event may be too personal or painful for a workshop participant to discuss.

After participants have completed this exercise, tell them to keep their copies handy during the workshop so they can add to their responses as the workshop progresses.

Ask workshop participants to think about why people need a workshop on stress. If time permits, ask participants to try to define stress. Their definitions may be recorded on a chalkboard, flipchart, or an overhead projector. Point out that people define stress in various ways, depending on their life experience and background. Ask participants to discuss what they mean when they say that "someone is under a lot of stress."

Defining Stress

People often use the term *stress* incorrectly. Many people equate being busy with being stressed. Although having a lot to do in a brief period may be stressful, feeling rushed is just one type of stress. Popular definitions of stress are very different from the scientific definition of stress. People often use the following terms to describe someone who is experiencing stress:

➤ *Tired:* emotionally and physically weary
➤ *Anxious:* nervous, feeling time constraints or pressure to perform, awareness of personal limits
➤ *Upset:* responding to a situation with anger or fear

The scientific/medical view of stress is more precise. After 30 years of stress research, Hans Selye published *The Stress of Life*.[1] Selye discovered that the human body's response to change is similar for many different kinds of change. He found this to be true regardless of whether the change is pleasant or painful. He concluded that whenever a person has to cope with change, the human body undergoes a *stress response*. Our responses vary with the situation, but different stressors elicit remarkably similar responses.

Briefly stated, we experience stress when we have to shift our emotional or physical gears. Examples of *stressors*—situations that require some kind of quick response—include the following:

➤ Physical danger, feeling unsafe and threatened
➤ Sudden changes in one's environment, such as heat, cold, pain, or some other discomfort

- ➤ Time pressures
- ➤ Having to make a transition from one setting or role to another, such as the transition from employee to parent after work
- ➤ Awareness of a serious problem, such as financial or family problems
- ➤ Illness or change in health status

Selye called the process by which a person's body adapts to these stressors a stress response. The stress response is a nonspecific or general response, in that the response occurs regardless of the stressor. Selye refers to the changes that occur in a person's body when he or she is under stress as the *general adaptation syndrome*.

General Adaptation Syndrome

Distribute the "What Is a Stress Response?" handout. Explain the stress-response model and the three stages of the general adaptation syndrome.

A stress response is triggered by a stressor event. Stress occurs when you perceive a need to cope with some physical or emotional change. Internal alarms go off as your body gets ready to deal with a stressor. When you choose a behavioral response (i.e., you decide to act in response to the stressor), you're responding externally. If the response reduces your stress level, then you may conclude that that behavior worked well for you. If your stress isn't reduced, you'll need to seek another response. This is called a "feedback loop"—the stressor affects you, and you try to affect the stressor. If you fail, you may seek another way to deal with the stressor.

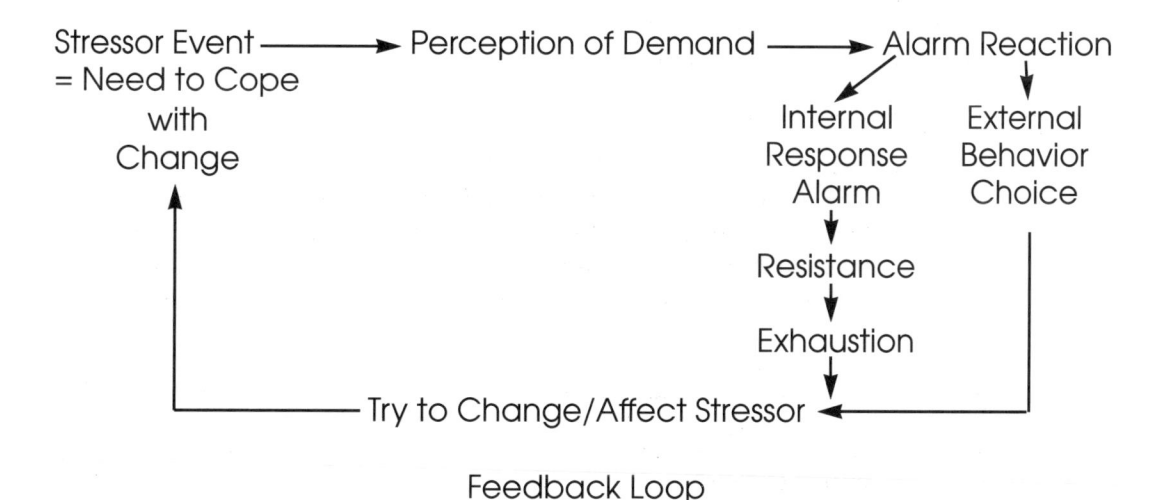

Stressor Event ⟶ Perception of Demand ⟶ Alarm Reaction

Internal Response Alarm

External Behavior Choice

Resistance

Exhaustion

⟵ Try to Change/Affect Stressor

Feedback Loop

Workplace Stress

Ask participants to refer to the "What Is a Stress Response?" handout.

Stress causes your body to go through a three-stage internal response called the *general adaptation syndrome*. This is an involuntary response. Some people can control their internal reactions to stress, but it requires training and practice.

The response starts with the perception of a need to cope with change. You hear, see, feel, or smell something that sets off an alarm reaction.

This syndrome has three stages. In the first stage, an *alarm* goes off in the brain (possibly in the hypothalamus) when a stressor is perceived. The alarm causes involuntary physiological changes within your body.

In the second stage (the *resistance* stage), the body readies itself to meet the emergency. Biochemical changes occur as the body attempts to adapt and to control possible damage caused by the stressor. Resisting a stressor can consume a lot of energy.

When the body is unable to resist or adapt any longer, the individual reaches the final stage of *exhaustion*. Exhaustion may result in serious illness, even death.

Selye describes two different kinds of *adaptation energy*:[2]

- Superficial adaptation energy is like having cash in your pocket. It's instantly available and may be replenished with a rest, nap, good night's sleep, or relaxing vacation.
- Deep adaptation energy may be compared with having 30-year treasury notes or bonds. It represents a reserve supply of energy that's available if needed to cope with major crises in one's life, but once it's exhausted, it's gone. It may take years for a person to recover from the expenditure of his or her deep adaptation energy.

Everyone Experiences Stress

We all experience stress; adults, children, even pets experience stress as a result of changes in their life. But compared with the research efforts that have focused on adults, little attention has been focused on how stress affects children. Questions about children and stress are difficult to answer without conducting an in-depth study of the child and his or her family.

Workshop participants who request more information about this topic can be directed to the following publications: Alice Sterling Honig, "Stress and Coping in Children," Young Children (May/July, 1986), pp. 50–63; Andrea Atkins, "Type-A Tots," Better Homes and Gardens (November 1989), p. 36.

Why People Respond Differently to Stress

People experience stress differently for several reasons. Selye identified conditioning factors that affect individuals' reactions to stress. These factors make a person more or less sensitive to stress and include both internal and external factors.
- Internally, you may have a genetic predisposition to respond in a particular way. Some research suggests that temperament is an inherited characteristic. How you respond to stress may also depend in part on your age, sex, and your past experience.
- External factors include medications, climate, and diet.

Although stressors can lead to a general response, they may also have specific effects on a person. For example, stress caused by the fear of losing your job may feel different from the way you feel when giving a speech. People also differ in their behavioral responses to stress, meaning that they select different types of behaviors that they think will help them cope with change.

The instructor may wish to ask workshop members to describe how they typically respond to stress.

There are no hard and fast rules regarding how people react to a stressor, but if we were to generalize, would you agree or disagree with the following statements?
- People have a tendency to choose the easiest, most familiar course of action.
- If offered a choice, most people will select a passive response over an active one.
- Most people try to avoid actions that expose their feelings and make them feel vulnerable.
- Most people choose simple solutions over complex ones. When faced with a stressful situation, people tend to look for the quickest and easiest way to resolve it.
- People usually try to avoid confrontations; they don't want to take risks (personal risks or risks to a relationship).
- Some people are always looking for a fight. They delight in having an excuse to show off and to express righteous indignation.

When a situation becomes stressful, we have a choice. We can decide to either (1) live with the stressor (a "syntoxic" response) or (2) fight against it and try to change it ("catatoxic" response).

Eastern and Western philosophic traditions view stress differently. In the West—especially in the United States—we believe that it's important to try to change things when they need changing. Eastern philosophers view life differently, as illustrated by the story of the willow and the oak:

Workplace Stress

> In a certain forest there stood a mighty oak and a fragile willow. A student was asked which of these was the greater and he replied, "Surely the oak is mightier than the willow. It has branches strong enough to support a man and a trunk thicker than three men."
>
> A fierce storm came along with howling winds that whipped through the forest. The oak resisted the gusts of wind for as long as it could. Finally, though, the gale ripped the oak up by the roots and threw it down.
>
> The fragile willow bent with the winds and bowed before the breeze. When the storm passed, the oak was down, but the "frail" willow was still standing.

This fable illustrates the choices we face in our response to stress:

- Should we resist, like the mighty oak, understanding that we don't have unlimited energy and that in the end we may well fail?
- Or should we bend like the frail willow, letting changes pass without fighting or resisting them?

Physicians use the medical term *dysponesis* (dis-poh-nee'-sis), which was coined by George Whatmore to describe "faulty trying" or "hard effort," to indicate what happens to people who try too hard to cope with stressful situations.[3] Dysponesis is a problem when it becomes a conditioned response to nearly every stressor. People who are dysponetic have difficulty relaxing. Dysponesis leads to early exhaustion and to a person feeling more helpless and less able to cope with a stressful situation.

Learning to accept the fact that some things can't be changed isn't easy. We live in a society that places a high value on being in control. We believe that we must take charge of the situation, assume power over our environment, and change whatever needs changing. We live in a "can-do" society in which very little is considered impossible.

Accepting human limitations, however, is part of the process of achieving maturity and wisdom. It doesn't mean giving up your youthful dreams and ideals, but it does mean deciding which battles are worth fighting and choosing how you will allocate your time, energy, and emotional commitments. Various factors affect our decisions on whether to act:

- A decision may be based on prior experiences—what has worked for you in the past.
- It may rest on your motivation—to what extent you feel you must deal with a stressor.
- It may depend on how much time and energy you have available to direct toward a solution.

Ask participants whether people would be better off with fewer changes in their lives. The following points can be incorporated into the discussion:

Workshop 1

- People need a certain level of intellectual, emotional, and physical stimulation in their lives.
- Lack of stimulation results in boredom; thus the flip side of burnout is "rustout."
- Change, *per se*, is not a bad thing; the problem is figuring out how to deal with changes when they occur.

Why Is Stress a Problem?

This portion of the workshop deals with how stress affects people's lives. Although much of this information has become common knowledge in the past few years, many people are not aware of the far-reaching effects of stress. The instructor should note that although stress may be associated with or linked to many illnesses, scientists are not able to state with confidence that stress causes a particular medical problem. Recent research indicates that stress is usually one of, and not necessarily the most important of, several causes of various medical problems. A workshop participant who expresses concern over a physical symptom or wants to know more about stress-related illnesses should be advised to see a physician.

Not all stress is bad. In fact, we all need some stress in our lives. In addition, it's hard, if not impossible, to avoid stress in the modern world.

Problems with stress arise when you have to deal with too much stress that lasts too long and when your "tools" for coping with stress are inadequate. That's when stress begins to affect your mental and physical health as well as your relationships.

Psychological Effects of Stress [4]

People who live with high stress over a long period find that gradually their adaptive and resistive abilities weaken until finally they reach the exhaustion stage. Psychologically, the person feels worn down, beaten, and emotionally weary.

If the strain becomes too great, you may seek escape, a way to avoid stress, and respite from your problems. You may feel a strong urge to run away from your troubles, become emotionally vulnerable, and wish to withdraw from others.

Stress can consume so much of your energy that you become apathetic toward others. High stress makes you feel helpless, sometimes causing you to regress to childish feelings and actions.

Stress can make you forgetful. You may have difficulty concentrating and become accident prone.

When under stress, you may become fearful and anxious. Body tension may even induce muscle cramps.

Workplace Stress

You may be easily startled. Nervous habits such as tics or giggling may become obvious, and compulsive behaviors may become more serious.

High stress is often associated with sleep disorders: insomnia, nightmares, narcolepsy.

Stress can affect your sex drive and eating patterns as well.

Our self-esteem is also affected by stress. If you feel that you are unable to control, fix, or change things, you may feel helpless, trapped, and stuck. You may become angry or feel weak, stupid, inadequate, and incompetent.

Physical Effects of Stress

Distribute the "Signs of Stress" handout. The instructor may choose to read from the handout at this point or go over the handout after the "Other Effects of Stress" section. The following lists some physical and psychological symptoms related to living with high levels of stress. Participants should check those items that apply to them.

1. General irritability, hyperexcitation, depression
2. Heart pounding, indicative of high blood pressure
3. Dryness of the mouth and throat
4. Impulsive behavior, emotional instability
5. Overpowering urge to cry or run or hide
6. Inability to concentrate, scattered thoughts, general disorientation
7. Feelings of unreality, weakness, or dizziness
8. Fatigue, loss of zest for life
9. "Floating" anxiety with no specific source of fear
10. Emotional tension, feeling hyperalert and keyed up
11. Trembling, nervous tics
12. Startle reactions
13. High-pitched giggle, nervous laughter
14. Stuttering, other speech problems
15. Bruxism (grinding one's teeth)
16. Insomnia or major changes in sleep patterns
17. Hyperactivity (difficulty relaxing)
18. Sweating
19. Frequent need to urinate
20. Digestive problems (diarrhea, indigestion, nausea)
21. Migraine headaches
22. Premenstrual tension, missed menstrual cycles
23. Neck or lower back pain
24. Diminished or excessive appetite for food
25. Increased use of tobacco, alcohol, or other drugs
26. Chemical addiction (alcoholism, drug addiction)

27. Nightmares
28. Neurotic behavior
29. Psychoses
30. Accident proneness

Stress and Relationships

Personal relationships can be both a source of strength as well as a drain on your resources. Although friends, family, co-workers, and others may offer support when your life becomes stressful, you may find it difficult to give people the attention they need if you are preoccupied with a stressful situation.

Developing healthy relationships with others requires concentration, time, and energy. When you are under a lot of stress, your attention may be focused on the source of that stress, rather than on interpersonal relations. It's very difficult to work on or maintain interpersonal relationships while you're under high stress.

People in high-stress occupations—medicine, counseling, nursing, social services, to name a few—may find that they give so much to the people with whom they work that they have little left for their friends and family members. (In fact, burnout is a long-term effect of working in such stressful occupations.)

Nearly everyone goes through stressful periods. People who are experiencing high levels of stress need to devote more time and energy to coping and problem solving and thus have little to offer others. Such periods in a person's life are understandable, but be wary of people who use stress as an excuse for *never* working on a relationship.

Other Effects of Stress

Various theories link stress to health and medical problems. However, evidence is still being gathered by researchers, who are examining the connections between stress and

- Hormonal changes (stress may affect testosterone and estrogen levels; aggressive behaviors may result from increased levels of testosterone)
- Premenstrual syndrome
- Reduced resistance to disease
- Cancer and heart disease, especially stress resulting from marital separation, divorce, or work problems[5]
- Arthritis[6]
- Other illnesses: digestive disorders, migraine headaches, diabetes, allergies

Researchers in the field of psychoneuroimmunology have found many examples of stress-related illnesses:

Workplace Stress

- Higher incidences of illness and accidents have been found among separated and divorced men and women.[7]
- The stock market crash in October 1987 has been tied to 116 cases of mumps among stockbrokers.

What Happens during a Stress Response?

Stress is sometimes referred to as the "fight or flight" response. Your body reacts to danger or the need to cope with change by getting ready to take action.

Stress researcher Richard Lazarus developed five categories of stress responses according to the action one chooses to deal with the stressor:[8]

- Flight in fear
- Fight in anger
- Immobility in panic: paralysis of thought or action
- Resourcefulness: converting a threat into a challenge
- Intrapersonal palliative strategies: reducing the threat in your mind

When the stress alarm goes off, physiological changes occur as your body gets ready for "fight or flight." One way to visualize what stress looks like is to imagine someone who is very angry. Anger is just one of several kinds of stress responses. What does someone who is enraged look like?

The instructor has several choices here: (1) Read through the exercise while participants fill in answers on their handouts, (2) have participants work through the exercise individually or as a group, or (3) ask participants to help identify how different parts of the body respond when a person gets angry. As participants provide answers, the instructor may try acting out how the body is getting ready to take action. Some participants, particularly those whose parents had trouble controlling anger, do not respond well to this demonstration. The instructor should attend carefully to participants' reactions.

- Hair: stands up, scalp tightens
- Eyes: grow larger and brighter, tears form, pupils dilate
- Face: flushed, sweaty
- Mouth: dry
- Neck: muscles tighten, hair on back of neck stands up
- Jaws: tightly clenched
- Shoulders: muscles tense
- Heart: pulse increases, blood pressure rises
- Lungs: respiration faster and shallower
- Liver: begins turning carbohydrates into usable sugars
- Stomach: digestion stops, muscles tense
- Muscles: tensed

Workshop 1

- Hands/feet: colder (slower circulation), fists clenched
- Perspiration: increases except for hands
- Senses: smell, taste, touch, sight, hearing much sharper
- Brain: shuts down, sympathetic nervous system takes over
- Voice pitch: higher, shriller
- Voice volume: louder, more emotional
- Mentation: difficult to think clearly, to talk sense

Overcoming Stress

All of the changes listed above result from the release of miniscule amounts of chemicals by the brain. If you do nothing, your body will neutralize and eliminate these chemicals over the course of three to four hours. Because these chemicals are so powerful, people who live with high stress are at risk for medical problems. Some researchers have also linked chemicals resulting from the stress response to aging.

Engaging in vigorous physical activity helps flush these chemicals out of your system fairly quickly. Other methods include relaxation techniques, meditation, and biofeedback. A list of ways to reduce the effects of stress on the body is given in the "Ways to Reduce the Effects of Stress" handout. It is important for all of us to have some way of dealing with stress.

You may reduce the effects of stress in your life in either of two ways. You may choose to learn to live with stress by finding a way to get your body back to normal as quickly as possible or you may decide to do something about the source of your stress. The latter method depends upon your being able to identify your stressors.

Some stressor events are pleasant—most are not. Stressors are often caused by demands on your time, energy, or intelligence. All stressors require you to shift gears emotionally and to cope with change.

Distribute the "Sources of Stress" handout and ask workshop participants to follow along.

Each stage of life has its accompanying stressors. These events are called *life-cycle stressors.* One way to measure stress is to examine the life stage and events a person is currently encountering.
- Moving from infancy to childhood
- Moving from adolescence to adulthood
- Dating, courtship, and marriage
- Separation and divorce
- Pregnancy and parenthood (raising children, letting them go)
- Job and career

- Death of parents
- Widowhood
- Aging, illness, infirmity

As we grow older, we experience challenges to and changes in our personal values and attitudes; we become more aware of our individual needs:

- Attitudes: liking or disliking what and who we are
- Self-expectations: feeling successful, capable, and competent; helpless or trapped; contented and happy
- Feelings: coping with strong emotions (both positive and negative)
- Expectations of others: getting along with others; coexisting with people who have different values

In addition, the physical changes, illnesses, and disabilities that accompany aging can be stressful.

Changes in society affect all of us. In the past few years, we have seen many changes in our families; our communities; and our economic, political, and legal environments:

- Maintaining our quality of life: economic pressures on wage earners, managers, business owners; urban sprawl and inner-city decay
- Environmental crises: hazardous waste; overpopulation and overcrowding; dwindling energy resources; commuting, parking, and transportation hassles
- World economy: competing and working with foreigners or people whose language and culture are very different from ours
- Technological changes
- Changing values: family composition and role definitions; social attitudes toward sex, role of women, parenting, drug and alcohol use and addictions, fear of sexually transmitted diseases

People are employed at jobs in the 1990s that didn't even exist 15–20 years ago. Many people experience tremendous pressure from their jobs and careers:

- Coping with expectations and disappointments: inadequate wages, feeling socially useful, monotony and boredom, unclear goals
- Managing conflict with co-workers and supervisors
- Transition from manufacturing to service economy
- Work overload and burnout
- Time pressures, deadlines
- Public attitudes and perceptions
- Trying to protect income and profits from the IRS
- Surviving takeovers, mergers, corporate raiders
- Foreign ownership of U.S. companies
- Relocation

Measuring stress in terms of life events was first done by Holmes and Rahe, who developed the Social Readjustment Rating Scale in 1967.[9] The scale rates the amount of stress, both positive and negative, that people experience from different life events. Even though the scale is outdated, many stress-management training programs still use it, because it demonstrates that both pleasant and unpleasant events can cause stress and logically indicates the degree of stress accompanying stressful situations.

Contemporary life has brought about new problems as well as a new openness about old problems. Today, people are more willing to discuss these problems, which makes them very hard to ignore, especially when many of them affect us personally:

- Increases in the crime rate mean that more people have had to deal with theft, assault, and fear.
- Television brings local, national, and international events into our homes. We are exposed to a constant stream of news reports on disasters, tragedies, wars, assassinations, kidnappings, and so forth.
- Some stressful events aren't experienced immediately. Sometimes people become victims of post-traumatic stress syndrome, for example, combat veterans or disaster victims.
- Family and love relationships have changed significantly over the past few decades. Today, more people live in single-parent and remarried or "blended" families. Studies have shown that the stress of marital separation and divorce has long-term negative effects for both adults and children.[10] Reports of family violence have become more prevalent: reported incidents of child abuse and incest have skyrocketed in recent years.
- Alcohol and other chemical dependency problems have a debilitating effect on family members.
- Teenage pregnancy has been recognized as a national problem.
- Homosexuality and alternative life-styles are no longer hidden from public view, a situation that some find very threatening.
- The threat of AIDS has generated public fear and animosity toward persons with HIV—or even toward people who *might* be infected.

Conclusion

Much of the research on stress is relatively new. We still don't know many things about the connections among mind, body, and emotions. We do know, however, that living with high stress for an extended period isn't good. Thus, it's important for us to understand how stress affects us and to find ways to cope better with stress. More extensive information on coping is presented in Workshop 2—Dealing with Job Stress.

Questions for workshop participants to consider:

- What has this workshop taught you about how stress affects your life?

- When you think about the stressors in your life and the tools you have for dealing with stress, are things better or worse than you thought when you decided to attend this workshop?
- Did you discover that you have more stress-related symptoms than you expected?
- Review the "Why Do You Need This Workshop?" handout. How do you feel now about the answers you gave at the start of the workshop?

References

1. Hans Selye, *The Stress of Life* (New York: McGraw-Hill, 1956).
2. Hans Selye, *Stress without Distress* (Philadelphia: J. B. Lippincott, 1974), p. 28.
3. George B. Whatmore and D. R. Kohli, *Dysponesis: A Neurophysiologic Factor in Functional Disorders*, in Erik Peper et al., eds., *Mind/Body Integration* (New York: Plenum Press, 1979).
4. C. Michele Haney and Edmond W. Boenish, Jr., *StressMap: Finding Your Pressure Points* (San Luis Obispo, CA: Impact Publishers, 1982), p. 7.
5. James J. Lynch, *The Broken Heart: Medical Consequences of Loneliness* (New York: Basic Books, 1979).
6. Frederick K. Goodwin, "Behavioral Stress Reactivity Related to Arthritis Susceptibility?" *Journal of the American Medical Association* 267 (February 1992): 910.
7. Gerald F. Jacobson, *The Multiple Crises of Marital Separation and Divorce* (New York: Grune and Stratton, 1982).
8. Richard Lazarus, *Patterns of Adjustment* (New York: McGraw-Hill, 1976).
9. Thomas H. Holmes and Richard H. Rahe, "Social Readjustment Rating Scale," *Journal of Psychosomatic Research* 2 (1967): 213–218.
10. Judith S. Wallerstein and Sandra Blakeslee, *Second Chances: Men, Women, and Children a Decade after Divorce* (New York: Ticknor & Fields, 1989).

Handout

Outline for Workshop 1

I. Introduction
II. Why a Workshop on Stress
   A. "Why Do People Need This Workshop" handout
   B. Preliminary definition of stress
III. Defining Stress
   A. Popular definitions of stress—tired, anxious, upset
   B. Scientific/medical view of stress
   C. Stress response
IV. General Adaptation Syndrome
   A. Feedback loop
      1. Stressor event
      2. Behavioral response
   B. Three-stage internal response
      1. Alarm
      2. Resistance
      3. Exhaustion
V. Why People Respond Differently to Stress
   A. Conditioning factors
      1. Internal: genetic predisposition
      2. External: medications, climate, diet
   B. Choices
      1. Syntoxic response: living with the stressor
      2. Catatoxic response: fighting against the stressor
   C. Dysponesis—"faulty trying" or "hard effort"
   D. Accepting human limitations
VI. Why Is Stress a Problem?
   A. Not all stress is bad
   B. Psychological effects of stress
   C. Physical effects of stress
   D. Stress and relationships
   E. Other effects of stress
VII. What Happens during a Stress Response?
   A. Flight
   B. Fight

        C. Immobility/panic
        D. Resourcefulness
        E. Intrapersonal palliative strategies
VIII. Overcoming Stress
        A. Living with stress
        B. Taking action against the source of stress
        C. Life-cycle stressors
            1. Developmental issues
            2. Challenges to personal values and attitudes
            3. Physical changes, illness, disability
            4. Societal changes
            5. Job and career pressures
IX. Conclusion

Handout

Why Do You Need This Workshop?

Where is the stress in your life coming from? List three people, places, or situations you associate with feeling stressed:

1. _____
2. _____
3. _____

How does it feel to be under stress? Describe five symptoms, feelings, or behaviors you associate with being stressed:

1. _____
2. _____
3. _____
4. _____
5. _____

What was the most stressful thing that ever happened to you? (This may be very personal; don't feel obligated to share your answer with others.)

_____
_____
_____
_____
_____

What tools do you have for dealing with stress? List three things you have done in the past to help you cope with stressful situations:

1. _____
2. _____
3. _____

Workplace Stress

Handout

What Is a Stress Response?

A stress response is set off by a *stressor*, an event that leads you to perceive a need to cope with some physical and/or emotional change. The stressor sets off an "alarm" in the brain, which in turn releases special chemicals. The chemicals cause changes in different parts of the body, preparing you to take action. This process is called the *general adaptation syndrome*.[1]

Alarm
- Goes off when brain perceives danger/threat
- Alarm set off, perhaps by the hypothalamus
- Physiological changes within body
- Involuntary, not something you can control

Resistance
- "Damage control," rushes to meet emergency
- Body adapts to change
- Mobilization of *adaptation energy* to resist

Exhaustion
- Unable to resist or adapt any longer

Stress Reactions

Five categories of stress reactions based on the action you take:[2]
- Flight: fear
- Fight: anger
- Immobility: panic, paralysis of thought or action
- Resourcefulness: seeking out resources, converting threat into challenge
- Intrapersonal palliative strategies: reducing the threat in your mind without reducing it in reality

1. Hans Selye, *Stress without Distress* (Philadelphia: J. B. Lippincott, 1974).
2. Richard Lazarus, *Patterns of Adjustment* (New York: McGraw-Hill, 1976).

Handout

Signs of Stress

____ General irritability, hyperexcitation, depression
____ Pounding of heart indicative of high blood pressure
____ Dryness of the mouth and throat
____ Impulsive behavior, emotional instability
____ Overpowering urge to cry or run and hide
____ Inability to concentrate, scattered thoughts, general disorientation
____ Feelings of unreality, weakness, or dizziness
____ Fatigue, loss of zest for living
____ "Floating" anxiety with no specific source of fear
____ Emotional tension, feeling hyperalert and keyed up
____ Trembling, nervous tics
____ Startle reactions
____ High-pitched giggle, nervous laughter
____ Stuttering, other speech problems
____ Bruxism (grinding one's teeth)
____ Insomnia or major change in sleep patterns
____ Hyperactivity (difficulty relaxing)
____ Sweating
____ Frequent need to urinate
____ Digestive problems (diarrhea, indigestion, nausea)
____ Migraine headaches
____ Premenstrual tension; missed menstrual cycles
____ Neck or lower back pain
____ Diminished or excessive appetite for food
____ Increased use of tobacco and alcohol
____ Increased use of medications (tranquilizers, sedatives, etc.)
____ Chemical addiction (alcoholism, drug addiction)
____ Nightmares
____ Neurotic behavior
____ Psychoses
____ Accidents

Adapted with permission from Hans Selye, *The Stress of Life*, rev. ed. (New York: McGraw-Hill, 1978), pp. 174–77.

Workplace Stress

Handout

What Does Stress Do to You?

Stress is sometimes called the "fight or flight" response, because your body reacts to danger or a need to cope with change. These physiological changes occur very quickly when you perceive a stressor.

What does stress look like?

Hair _____

Eyes _____

Mouth _____

Jaws _____

Neck _____

Heart _____

Lungs _____

Liver _____

Stomach _____

Hands/feet _____

Smell, sight, touch, taste, hearing _____

Face _____

Muscles _____

Voice _____

Brain _____

Is this a good time to try to win a "well-reasoned" debate?

Handout

Sources of Stress

Life cycle: Each stage of life has its accompanying stressors:
- Growing up: Transitions from infancy to childhood, adolescence to adulthood, etc.
- Dating, courtship, and marriage
- Separation and divorce
- Pregnancy and parenthood: Raising children, letting them go (empty nest), grandparenting
- Job and career: Training for and starting out in the work world, job hunting, unemployment, advancement/promotion, retirement
- Deaths of parents
- Widowhood
- Aging: Illness, infirmity

Personal: Changes in your values and attitudes, awareness of your needs and limitations:
- Attitudes: Liking (or disliking) what and who you are
- Expectations of yourself: Feeling successful, capable, and competent; feeling helpless or trapped; finding contentment and happiness
- Feelings: Coping with strong emotions (both positive and negative)
- Expectations of others: Getting along with others and resolving conflicts, coexisting with people who have different values

Social: Changes affecting family; community; economic, political, legal environments:
- Maintaining quality of life
- Economic pressures
- Urban sprawl; inner-city decay
- Environmental crises: Hazardous waste, uncertainty concerning energy sources, overpopulation, parking and transportation
- World economy
- Technological changes
- Values: Changing composition and definitions of "family"; new social attitudes toward sex, roles of women and men, aging, parenting, drug and alcohol use

Job and career: Many jobs of the 1990s didn't even exist 15–20 years ago:
- Expectations and disappointments: Getting more than money from a job, feeling socially useful, monotony and boredom, unclear goals
- Managing conflict with co-workers and supervisors
- Transition from manufacturing to service economy
- Work overload and burnout
- Time pressures, deadlines
- Public attitudes and perceptions
- Takeovers, mergers, corporate raiders
- Foreign ownership of U.S. companies
- Relocation

Physical: Living with an aging body can be stressful in that one may become more susceptible to disability, illnesses, and injuries.

Handout

Bibliography

Benson, Herbert (1975). *The Relaxation Response.* New York: William Morrow and Co.

Brown, Barbara (1977). *Stress and the Art of Biofeedback.* New York: Bantam Books.

Haney, C. Michele, & Boenish, Edmond W., Jr. (1982). *Stressmap: Finding Your Pressure Points.* San Luis Obispo, CA: Impact Publishers.

Jacobson, Edmund (1929). *Progressive Relaxation.* Chicago: University of Chicago Press.

Jacobson, Edmund (1978). *You Must Relax.* New York: McGraw-Hill.

Lazarus, Richard (1976). *Patterns of Adjustment.* New York: McGraw-Hill.

Lynch, James T. (1979). *The Broken Heart: Medical Consequences of Loneliness.* New York: Basic Books.

McCubbin, Hamilton I., & Figley, Charles I. (Eds.) (1983). *Stress and the Family: Coping with Normative Transitions* (Vols. 1 and 2). New York: Brunner/Mazel.

Selye, Hans (1956). *The Stress of Life.* New York: McGraw-Hill.

Selye, Hans (1974). *Stress without Distress.* Philadelphia: J. B. Lippincott.

Sparks, James Allen (1982). *Living the Bad Days: Why They Come and How to Survive.* Nashville, TN: Abingdon Press.

Stroebel, Charles F. (1982). *QR: The Quieting Reflex.* New York: G. P. Putnam's Sons.

Whatmore, George B., & Kohli, D. R. (1979). *Dysponesis: A Neurophysiologic Factor in Functional Disorders.* In Erik Peper et al. (Eds.), *Mind/Body Integration.* New York: Plenum Press.

Williams, Redford (1989). *The Trusting Heart: Great News about Type A Behavior.* New York: Times Books.

For additional information about stress and related subjects, write or call:

The American Institute of Stress
124 Park Avenue
Yonkers, NY 10703
(914) 963-1200

Workplace Stress

Handout

Ways to Reduce the Effects of Stress

A couple of basic methods can be helpful in coping with stress. First, respond directly to the stressor—try to change the situation or deal with the person who is creating stress. Attempt to convince others that change is both desirable and feasible.[1]

Second, reduce the effects of stress on your body and mind. The following lists some ways people counter the physiological effects of stress. One method or the other may work for you, depending on whether you primarily experience stress mentally, physically, or in combination.

Mental Stress
- Read Herbert Benson's *The Relaxation Response* (see "Stress Resources" handout).
- Learn Hatha Yoga, a regimen of breathing, exercise, diet, and meditation.
- Try deep breathing, using visualization techniques to reduce tension and distract the mind.
- Read Edmund Jacobson's *You Must Relax* (see "Stress Resources" handout) to learn progressive relaxation with visualization.
- Self-distract by concentrating on a book, game, etc.
- Do some physical exercise that requires concentration.
- Systematically desensitize yourself by gradually replacing anxiety with relaxation.
- Self-hypnotize by using suggestive words or phrases that help you relax.
- Use guided self-dialogue by talking yourself through stress-producing situations.

Physical
- Learn how to do deep muscle relaxation (read Edmund Jacobson's *You Must Relax* or Charles Stroebel's *Quieting Reflex*) (see "Stress Resources" handout).
- Read Edmund Jacobson's *You Must Relax* to learn progressive relaxation with visualization.
- Meditate (concentrate, refocus your energy).
- Yoga.
- Massage.
- Physical exercise.

Physical and Mental
- Vigorous exercise.
- Sports or activities that require deep concentration.

The following do *not* reduce stress (and might make things worse):
- Alcohol.
- Drugs (even some prescription medicines).
- Binging—on food or drink.
- Refined sugar.
- Television (commercials are designed to stimulate and arouse, not relax).
- Going for a drive (very dangerous when you have trouble concentrating).

The following might help (and won't make things worse)
- Soak in a hot tub or take a shower, go for a swim, use a shower-massager.
- Hot tea or cocoa (without sugar)—these are psychologically soothing drinks for many people.
- Learn biofeedback—with proper training, biofeedback techniques can help you control stress responses.
- Psychotherapy—especially with a group of people in similar situations.
- Escape—only works if it is predictable, truly "away" from stressors, lasts long enough to let you recharge your batteries.

1. For more information on this approach, see Steven B. Zwickel, *Anger* (Milwaukee, WI: Family Service America, Inc., 1992), p. 105.

Workplace Stress

Handout

Evaluation Form

This workshop offers participants basic information about stress. Participants learn to recognize sources of stress and how stress affects them—psychologically, physically, and in their relationships with others.

Learning Objectives:
- To provide participants with a better sense of what professionals mean when they talk about stress.
- To demonstrate how stress derives from various sources.
- To help participants understand the effects of stress.

Please respond to these questions by circling the answers you agree with. Your comments will be used to help improve future programs.

1. The presenter fulfilled my expectations of what I wanted to learn from this workshop.

    Very much   Pretty much   Somewhat   Not at all

    Comments:_____
    _____
    _____
    _____

2. I can use the information I obtained in this workshop in my job and/or personal relations.

    Very much   Pretty much   Somewhat   Not at all

    Comments:_____
    _____
    _____
    _____

3. The presenter knew the material, was organized, and presented the information clearly.

   Very much   Pretty much   Somewhat   Not at all

   Comments: _____
   _____
   _____
   _____

4. What would you have liked the presenter to do differently?
   _____
   _____
   _____
   _____

5. What did you like most about this workshop?
   _____
   _____
   _____
   _____

Workshop 2

➤ Dealing with Job Stress

Learning Objectives

- ➤ To help participants understand the relationship between different sources of stress in the workplace.
- ➤ To explain research findings regarding the Type-A personality.
- ➤ To explore options for dealing with job stress.

Introduction

This workshop examines stress in the workplace. It covers some of the most common stressors found on the job and looks at the stress problems faced by people with Type-A personalities.

"Dealing with Job Stress" continues (without duplicating) the previous workshop, "Introduction to Stress." In addition to exploring the relationship between stress and the workplace, it also demonstrates the connections among stress, anger, time management, burnout, and competitiveness. Thus it can be used as an extended introduction to the workshops for these topics.

Handouts

- ➤ Workshop Outline
- ➤ Why Do You Work?

Workplace Stress

- What's Stressful about Work?
- Workplace Sources of Job Stress
- Dealing with Job Stress
- Evaluation Form

Why Do We Work?

After introductions have been made, explain the format of the workshop and distribute "Workshop Outline" and "Why Do You Work?" handouts. The "Why Do You Work?" handout serves as a good warm-up exercise by helping participants see that they work for reasons other than the simplistic explanation: "Primarily, for money." By going through the checklist, participants begin to see that they have other expectations of work beyond the need for a paycheck that may contribute to the stress they feel in the workplace.

What are some of the other reasons we spend 40-plus hours out of every 168-hour week working?

- Self-esteem: People work because it makes them feel good about themselves.
- Feeling useful: Work can be an important outlet for people's need to contribute to society.
- Helping: Many people have a need to help others through their work.
- Recognition: Some people want others to know and appreciate what they do; work may be a means to achieve fame.
- Power: Some people have a need to be in charge; the workplace offers them an arena in which they are able to assume a leadership role.
- Independence: Some jobs encourage and reward initiative, enabling a person to control his or her destiny.
- Fun: When work is something you enjoy doing, it can be fun.
- Sense of accomplishment: People feel good about themselves when they can take credit for having finished or built something of value.
- Self-exploration: Work may allow a person to learn more about him- or herself and the world.
- Avoiding guilt: Some people would feel immoral and bad if they did not work.
- Stimulation: Work offers those who might otherwise stay home a chance to meet interesting people or do interesting things.
- Approval of others: Working can help keep family members and others happy and not critical of the worker.

Whereas our ancestors had to struggle just to survive, times have changed and many people have diverse expectations of work. Social programs protect us so that we no longer have to work just for survival. Because we all expect different things from work, our motivations for work

Workshop 2

may result in confusion. In other words, it has become impossible to say, "This is what work *should* be!"

What we can say for sure, however, is that (1) more people are working today outside the home than ever before, and (2) the number of people who are dissatisfied and unhappy with their work seems to be growing. Part of this dissatisfaction with work is undoubtedly the failure of various jobs to live up to workers' expectations. Another part may be attributed to stress.

Stress in the Workplace

In the "Introduction to Stress" workshop, participants were given a brief overview of how we define stress, what causes it, and some techniques for coping with stress.

- Stress is the term used to describe how the human body responds when attacked or required to adapt to a physical or psychological change. The events or circumstances that cause this response are called stressors. Stressors may be pleasant or unpleasant.
- Stress is more than merely feeling rushed or overworked; it involves biochemical changes that affect the entire body. It can take the body several hours to get back to normal after a stress response.
- Problems arise when a person has to live with high levels of stress for an extended period. After the "stress alarm" goes off, the body deals with the stressor by resisting it. When a person's energy is depleted, the body reaches a stage of exhaustion.
- Stress can affect people both psychologically and physically. It has been linked to serious medical problems and to a higher risk of illness and accident.
- One way to measure stress is to look at the various stressors in a person's life. If you understand where stress is coming from, you can choose to deal with the stressor or find a way to live with it. Most jobs have some aspects that are stressful.

The following exercise will help participants identify stressors in the workplace. Draw a large "T" on a flip chart or chalkboard. Label one side "BEST" and the other side "WORST." Distribute the "What's Stressful about Work?" handout. Ask participants to jot down the characteristics of the best and worst jobs they ever had. Participants may want to look at these attributes in terms of people (superiors, subordinates, co-workers, customers), the job itself (tasks and responsibilities), the environment, and attitudes (of co-workers, managers, customers, suppliers). Ask volunteers to contribute items to the "T" on the board. Write each item on the appropriate side of the "T." Leave the chart up during the remainder of the session so participants can compare their experiences with the information provided in the workshop as it proceeds. Discussion of their responses might touch on the following.

- What makes some jobs so much better/worse than others?
- How do actual work experiences compare with expectations employees may have had before they started?
- Is there any way to spot a good/bad job situation before you start? What clues can you look for?

Myths regarding Money and Stress

Some people believe that if they make enough money, any amount of stress can be tolerated. Others conclude that because wealthy people have less to worry about, they experience less stress in their lives.

Although there may be some truth in these beliefs, it's misleading to make such generalizations. To debunk the first myth, one need only look at the lives of many of today's athletes and entertainers who earn millions, yet turn to drugs and alcohol in order to cope with stress.

As for the second myth, although it may be true that financial security relieves certain situations that cause stress, many wealthy people run businesses and work very hard to protect their investments. Wealth isn't a cure-all for stress.

Getting Along with People

Dealing with people in the workplace can be very stressful. In nearly every job, you must be able to get along with others. In the workplace, you are expected to respect and defer to your superiors and adapt to others' preferred styles of working. Team players and pursuit of organizational goals are valued. In other words, part of your job is to get along with others.

Playing by the Rules

Working for, with, or over other people means that you must *communicate* with them—exchange ideas, instructions, and feelings. With friends and family members you can "let your hair down" and be yourself. In the workplace, interactions are more formal and are expected to follow certain unwritten rules of behavior. These rules regulate how and with whom you communicate. They serve an important function in that they permit the conduct of business regardless of personal considerations. You may dislike, even despise, the people you work with, but because of these rules, you keep your mouth shut and work proceeds.

Some people might argue that this system of rules doesn't allow you to express yourself without restraint and thus is a demeaning form of servitude. Others might contend that regardless of personal feelings, you need to learn to live with these rules. An obvious advantage of such rules is that, if they are applied fairly, they promote equal treatment among workers.

The rules of the workplace may require you to adapt to other peoples' values and expectations. For example, compare how you talk and act when your boss or supervisor is around with how you behave on the telephone with a demanding customer or in a meeting with a high-pressure sales rep. In each of these situations you adapt; you may feel one way, yet you behave another way.

Interpersonal Communication

In any organization, it is important for individuals to be able to communicate clearly and easily with one another and with people outside the organization. Unfortunately, this doesn't always occur in the workplace. Communications can be a source of stress when they leave one person confused as to what was meant, unsure of what decision was made, angry over apparent injustices, or upset about being treated like a child. The following provides some examples of communication in the workplace and how such communication can be helpful or stressful:

- Job descriptions: Helpful if they define what a person is supposed to be doing with his or her time. Stressful if they're unclear and if responsibilities are blurred.
- Organizational charts: Helpful if they show how the different components of the workplace fit together. Stressful if they hide incompetence or make people feel small and unimportant.
- Newsletters: Helpful if they report on what's really going on in the organization (they seldom do). Stressful when they are the primary (or only) source of news within the organization. An error in a newsletter can damage someone's reputation or negatively affect the public's perceptions of an organization.
- Manuals: Helpful if they explain how to operate equipment or respond to a particular situation. Stressful if they are overly technical or if they are old and outdated.
- Policy decisions: Helpful if they provide direction to the organization. Stressful if handed down from above, with no discussion, no follow through, no explanation offered. Stressful if people do not receive official notification of changes and how to implement them. Stressful if policies are contradicted by practices.
- Meetings: Minutes can be helpful if they record decisions that were made and are distributed widely. Stressful if they are unproductive or used as a forum for blaming people.
- Faxes: Helpful in providing written records. Stressful if they make previously garbled communication even more confusing.

- ➤ Memos: Helpful if they record an opinion or decision. Stressful if they hide problems, shift blame, and avoid responsibility.
- ➤ Reports: Helpful if they give the reader a better understanding of what and how the organization is doing. Stressful if people are pressured to write reports that no one ever reads.

"Wearing" Your Workplace Attitude

More of us now work in service jobs in which we get paid for providing a service (as opposed to creating a product). In these jobs, people are paid to perform in particular ways.

Your "workplace attitude," which may be very different from the "real you," is an integral part of the job. However, if your "workplace attitude" doesn't fit your personality, your job may generate a lot of stress as you struggle to adapt.[1]

The instructor might ask participants to share examples of "workplace attitudes" that they wear or have worn. Follow up by asking if the person felt comfortable or stressed in that role.

Some examples of "workplace attitudes" include customer service representatives who are expected to be friendly, attentive, and encouraging with every customer or a collection agency employee who is supposed to be forceful, aggressive, and intimidating.

Anger

Another source of stress in the workplace is *anger*, both your own and other people's. Anger is not acceptable in the workplace. The rules of the workplace require you to maintain control of your feelings. Regardless of the situation, you're not permitted to express your anger. At best, displays of temper may subject you to ridicule or pity. At worst, you may be suspended or fired for "shooting your mouth off."

When people have no legitimate way to express their anger and outrage, anger is generally expressed in other ways—sabotage, lack of cooperation, low morale, and back-stabbing.

In some service jobs, stress stems from having to deal with angry people. It isn't easy for customer service representatives to listen to the outraged rantings of unhappy customers and then respond calmly and cheerfully, but that's what they're expected to do. Quality control of products helps reduce this kind of stress—the better the product, the less likely consumers will be dissatisfied.

Time-Management Issues

Stress in the workplace may also be the result of time-management issues. The fact that people work at different speeds with unclear priorities sets the stage for friction in the workplace. Having to rush or to accommodate other people's schedules can be extremely stressful.

Researchers have identified two keys to work stress—predictability and control—both of which directly affect how you spend your time. Laboratory experiments have shown that high-stress jobs are most frequently those in which you never know what's going to happen next and you have little or no control over your work.

Dealing with People

Some jobs require working primarily with numbers and figures; other jobs involve producing or manufacturing goods. Still other jobs entail developing and communicating ideas. Jobs that are "people-centered" have a high level of stress.

When people enter these jobs, they often do so with high expectations, energy, and enthusiasm. Over the course of time, unless they are careful about self-monitoring, that initial idealism starts to fade. Work becomes a place where they are constantly giving to others and getting little in return. They start feeling overwhelmed and unable to keep up. The long-term result of this is "burnout"—good people who no longer care, are no longer interested, who ask only for a paycheck and to be left alone.

Although burnout has several different causes, stress plays a significant role. The unrelenting, high levels of stress in people-centered jobs can lead to emotional exhaustion and burnout. Every year, many experienced teachers, nurses, physicians, counselors, and others drop out of their professions because they are too emotionally exhausted to continue.

Attitudes Affect Job Stress

Some of us love our work, some hate it, most fall somewhere in between. Our attitudes toward the work itself, the people with and for whom we work, and the work environment affect the level of stress we experience on the job.

How do you feel about money, credit, debt? Some people find it very difficult to talk about these subjects. They may be too embarrassed to discuss how much money they make or how much they owe. People's attitudes toward money affect the amount of stress they feel about working for money.

Workplace Stress

Being in debt makes some people feel guilty. They have strong feelings about not owing money to others. What happens to these people in an age in which just about everyone has at least one credit card? How do they feel about working to pay off credit-card debts? School loans? A home mortgage?

Other attitudes can add to stress. Some people resent having to work for other people or become jealous when others receive more money, praise, or perks, even when these rewards are earned or deserved. Others become angry over the many injustices they see in the work world: Even after years of trying to ensure fairness, discrimination, favoritism, and inequality still exist in the workplace.

The emphasis on speed and quality service in some occupations makes some people feel rushed and uncomfortable. They may feel as though they are being exploited. Or they may feel that their employer is patronizing or views employees as interchangeable parts.

The Modern Workplace and Stress

A major contributor to job stress is the physical work environment itself. Working in a noisy, dirty, uncomfortable environment can add significantly to your stress level.

Distribute "Workplace Sources of Job Stress" handout. Participants can go through this list on their own, or the instructor can use the handout as a class exercise. Each item on the handout can be rated subjectively along a scale from more stressful to less stressful. By going through the entire list, participants will be better able to identify sources of stress in their workplace.

How Does Your Workplace Measure Up?

Getting to Work
- Commuting: Is it easy or difficult for you to get to work?
- If you drive to work, is parking easy or difficult?

Work Environment
- Air quality: Many businesses today have a climate-controlled environment. Cigarette smoking may be prohibited or permitted only in certain areas. Is the air where you work fresh or stale? Are the heating and air-conditioning systems adequate and reliable or do the temperature and humidity fluctuate widely?
- Lighting: Is the lighting adequate for performing your work? If you work at a computer terminal, is glare a problem?
- Workplace: Is your work area kept clean? Does your work area have comfortable furnishings? Are you able to have privacy when you need it?

- Restrooms: Are the toilets and sinks clean and sanitary?
- Break room: Is the break room clean and attractive?

Office
- Noise: A big contributor to stress in the workplace is noise. How would you assess the effect of people talking, equipment sounds, distractions such as radios or Muzak in your workplace? Is the work area comfortably quiet or uncomfortably noisy?
- Office supplies: Are your supplies new and usable or old, broken, or nonexistent?
- Telephone: Is your system updated and reliable? Is the system noisy?

Plant
- Machine noise: Heavy machinery in a plant is relatively noisy. Because manufacturers are aware of the effects of noise on workers, newer equipment often comes with sound dampeners. Would you consider your plant uncomfortably noisy?
- Machinery: Is it new, working, and reliable or old, broken, or nonexistent?
- Maintenance: Is preventive maintenance performed on equipment or are repairs ordered only after a breakdown? Is the work performed by professionals? Is safety emphasized or are shortcuts encouraged?
- Work area: An area that's kept clean, safe, and unobstructed is much less stressful.
- Materials: Stress can result from having to locate materials in a dirty and poorly organized storage area.
- Vehicles: Are company cars, trucks, and so forth kept clean, maintained, and reliable?

Video Display Terminals

A great deal of attention has been focused on the possible dangers of video display terminals (VDTs) in the workplace. San Francisco went so far as to pass a city ordinance regulating the use of VDTs in business. The Occupational Safety and Health Administration (OSHA) distributes a free booklet titled *Working Safely with Video Display Terminals* (OSHA 3092). You can obtain a copy by writing to: OSHA, U.S. Department of Labor, Technical Data Center, Room N2439, 200 Constitution Avenue, N.W., Washington, DC 20210.

Some medical and psychological problems have been blamed on VDTs:
- Eyestrain: This can result from the video screen glare or poor positioning of the screen, improper lighting, or difficult-to-read copy material. The National Institute for Occupational Safety and Health (NIOSH) recommends 15-minute breaks every two hours for persons whose jobs require moderate use of computers. For high-level computer use or repetitive tasks, NIOSH recommends a 15-minute break after one hour of computer use.[2]

Workplace Stress

- Fatigue and repetitive motion syndrome: VDT operators are at risk of developing cumulative trauma or repetitive motion disorders such as carpal tunnel syndrome, a condition that can result in numbness, tingling, or severe pain in the wrist and hand. New ergonomic keyboards are designed to reduce this problem.
- Radiation: Experts disagree about whether VDT operators are exposed to harmful levels of radiation. Early studies reported a connection between VDT use and miscarriage and birth defects.[3] To date, however, there is no conclusive evidence that the low levels of radiation emitted by computer terminals are dangerous. The Occupational Safety and Health Administration is still investigating VDT radiation for harmful side effects. Persons who work at computer terminals should keep abreast of changing safety recommendations in computer-user magazines and national news reports.
- Back and shoulder pain: May be the result of poor work-station design or sitting incorrectly while working at a keyboard.
- Psychological stress: Although some people believe that working at a computer terminal is very stressful, evidence does not suggest that a properly designed work station is more stressful than other work stations. Electronic monitoring to count operators' keystrokes and production undoubtedly creates stress.

If you use a VDT in your work, be informed and be careful. Guidelines for the safe operation of VDTs are available from the manufacturer, your regional OSHA office, and computer-user and popular health magazines.

Type-A Behavior Patterns

Some people experience greater job stress than do others. In the 1960s, Meyer Friedman and Ray Rosenman followed 3,000 healthy, middle-aged men for eight and a half years. At the start of this study, Friedman and Rosenman did structured interviews with each participant. After analyzing the results of these interviews, they classified the men as either "Type A" or "Type B." Approximately half of the subjects were placed in each class.[4]

Typical Type-A behavior was characterized as follows:
- Speaking and moving emphatically and vigorously
- Strong sense of time urgency, impatience
- Hostile, aggressive, ambitious, and competitive

Friedman and Rosenman hypothesized that Type-A behavior might be linked to medical problems. By 1975, they concluded that Type-A persons were twice as likely to have heart disease symptoms as were Type Bs. In 1981, Type-A behavior was officially added to the list of medical causes of heart disease, joining smoking, hypertension, and others.

Workshop 2

Recent research has refined the original characteristics used by Friedman and Rosenman to define Type-A behavior. In addition to the traits listed above, Type-A behavior includes the following characteristics:
- Polyphasic thought or activity (often trying to do more than one thing at a time)
- Poor attending skills (not a good listener)
- Feeling guilty when relaxing
- Oblivious to activities outside work
- Preoccupied with possessions (materialistic, concerned with symbols of success)
- Nervous gestures, tics
- When asked, attributing success to speed
- Concerned with data and numbers (tending to ignore feelings, emotional responses, etc.)[5]

On the other hand, a Type-B person was originally characterized as someone who is free of Type-A behaviors, especially time urgency and free-floating hostility. Type Bs were viewed as being able to play, have fun, relax.

Type-A Personality and Hostility

Recent research in the field of behavioral medicine criticizes Friedman and Rosenman's original study, arguing that their original definition of Type-A personality was too broad. Researchers now believe it is possible to identify a person prone to heart disease by means of fewer and simpler criteria. In particular, researchers have been looking at the role of *hostility* in defining Type-A behavior.[6]

Hostility, for our purposes, is defined as having a strong, cynical mistrust of people. In addition to this underlying hostility, Type-A personality is marked by:
- Cynicism: Belief that other people are inherently bad, selfish, mean, and not to be trusted
- Hostile affect: Angry feelings when negative expectations of others are fulfilled
- Aggressive responses: Expression of anger through aggression directed toward others

Researchers are still studying the connection between stress and Type-A behavior to try to predict who is likely to suffer health problems. We do know the following:
- Type As have inadequate skills for coping with stress. Their biochemical makeup appears to intensify the effects of the stress response and it takes them longer to recover after a stress response.
- There may be markers of Type-A behavior other than time urgency or

Workplace Stress

hostility, such as perfectionism.
- Type As tend to die younger than do Type Bs.
- The stress response results in an increase in the secretion of the hormone testosterone in both men and women. Increased levels of testosterone is associated with aggressiveness, and higher levels of testosterone have been found in Type-A individuals. However, we don't know whether increased testosterone levels cause a person to become a Type A or whether Type-A behavior results in increased levels of testosterone.[7]

From Type A to Type B

The personality traits that are used to define someone as a Type-A personality are the very ones that lead to success in our society. The drive, ambition, and aggressiveness of Type As can lead to wealth and success. Many successful people in law, medicine, politics, sports, business, and entertainment are Type As.

Thus, it should come as no surprise that many Type As resist the idea of changing, even when they realize that their life-style puts them at risk. They may be afraid that changing will cause them to lose their competitive edge. Many Type As feel invincible, that they can continue to beat the odds. Unfortunately, for some Type As, it may take a heart attack to get the message across that they can't.

It is possible for a Type-A person to develop a Type-B life-style. The process begins with learning how to cope better with stress. If stress can be controlled, a Type-A person can learn to reduce his or her hostility—and consequently its effects on the body—as well as learn to trust people.

Type As have to make a conscious decision to slow their pace. They must learn to walk, speak, and eat more slowly. They must learn to add joy and laughter to their lives. They must learn how to delegate responsibility and to overcome their perfectionism, how to rest and relax without feeling guilty.

One way to change behavior involves working your way through the following 12 steps:[8]
- Reduce your cynical mistrust of others:
    1. Monitor your thoughts; keep a "hostility log."
    2. Tell people that you are working on reducing your hostility.
    3. Learn to "short-circuit" yourself when your mind starts racing.
- Reduce the level and intensity of strong negative emotions:
    4. Try to reason with yourself; be logical and rational.
    5. Imagine yourself in the other person's spot; learn to feel empathy for others.
    6. Learn to laugh at yourself; look for the humor in situations.

7. Find a tool to reduce your level of stress; relax.
➤ Learn to treat others with kindness and consideration, reserving assertiveness or aggression for situations in which they are really required:
8. Make friends and start trusting people.
9. Attend to what other people say; listen.
10. Substitute assertiveness for aggression.
11. Behave as though each day were your last.
12. Practice forgiveness; don't forget to forgive yourself.

Those of us who are not Type As have a vested interest in wanting Type As to change. Type As can spread misery wherever they go. Their demands for speed and perfection can drive their co-workers, employees, friends, and family up the wall.

Ask participants whether they identify with the characteristics of Type-A behavior. They may be able to provide examples of Type-A behavior that reinforce the material covered in this workshop. Those who live or work with Type As may wish to discuss ways to handle stressful confrontations with Type-A persons.

It isn't easy to change patterns developed over a lifetime. Talking about the dangers of Type-A behavior may motivate some workshop participants to seek help. Fortunately, resources are available:

➤ Reading materials: Most libraries and bookshops have books on stress reduction and health. The "Bibliography" handout lists various titles. Many others are available; ask your librarian for help.
➤ Medical problems: High levels of stress can lead to serious illness. Many clinics, health maintenance organizations, and hospitals offer programs and classes for people who want to change their Type-A behavior.
➤ Psychological help: Psychological profiles of Type-A people show that many of them are unhappy and disappointed with their lives. Counseling and group sessions with people who have similar problems can be very effective in helping Type As change.

Conclusion

It isn't possible to solve all the problems associated with stress in the workplace in a brief workshop such as this. The most we can hope to do is make people aware that they have choices and provide them with information that allows them to make informed decisions.

Distribute the "Dealing with Job Stress" handout. Participants can use this handout as a tool for solving problems. This exercise can be time consuming, so make sure that par-

ticipants understand the instructions for filling it in before they begin. If they don't have time to complete it during the workshop, they can take it home with them.

Begin by identifying *sources* of job stress. The other handouts distributed during the workshop should provide enough material to make this a fairly simple task.

Now, look for *patterns* among those sources to see if you can trace job stress to a particular person, place, time, task, or attitude at work.

Next, consider what would happen if you decided to *do nothing* about job stressors. Not taking action requires a decision and has its own set of consequences.

If you decide that some action is necessary, think about what will be required of you. Solutions may be categorized as:

➤ Some basic things you may be able to do to make your workplace less stressful: Finding ways to reduce noise, dirt, danger; taking better care of yourself through rest, diet, exercise, relaxation; stimulating yourself with outside interests.

➤ More complicated steps requiring some cooperation from boss and co-workers include replacing broken or obsolete equipment, making job responsibilities more equitable, clarifying communications.

➤ Very stressful situations may require major changes, such as trying not to be a Type A or a perfectionist, asking for a transfer, quitting your job, or changing careers.

Encourage participants to find creative solutions to problems caused by stress in the workplace. The instructor can conclude by having participants imagine themselves running businesses of their own and that one of their employees was attending a workshop on stress in the workplace. Ask participants, "What would you want your employee to say about you?"

References

1. Arlie Russell Hochschild, *The Managed Heart: Commercialization of Human Feeling* (Berkeley, CA: University of California Press, 1983).
2. Occupational Safety and Health Administration, *Working Safely with Video Display Terminals* (OSHA 3092) (Washington, DC: U.S. Department of Labor, 1991), p. 2.
3. Wendy Taylor, "VDT Hazards: Keep the Monitor Emissions at Arm's Length," *PC-Computing* 6 (January 1992), p. 250; J. Donald Miller (Director, National Institute for Occupational Safety and Health), prepared testimony before the House Subcommittee on Health and Safety (May 15, 1984), p. 9.
4. Meyer Friedman and Ray Rosenman, *Type A Behavior and Your Heart* (New

York: Alfred A. Knopf, 1974), pp. 86–87.
5. Ibid., pp. 82–85.
6. Redford Williams, *The Trusting Heart: Great News about Type A Behavior* (New York: Times Books, 1989), p. 71.
7. Theodore D. Kemper, *Social Structure and Testosterone: Explorations of the Socio-bio-social Chain* (New Brunswick, NJ: Rutgers University Press, 1990), p. 32.
8. Williams, *The Trusting Heart: Great News about Type A Behavior.*

Workplace Stress

Handout

Outline for Workshop 2

I. Introduction
II. Why Do We Work?
   A. Diverse expectations of work
   B. "Why Do You Work?" handout
III. Stress in the Workplace
   A. Defining stress
   B. Stress and work
   C. Myths regarding money and stress
   D. Getting along with people
   E. Playing by the rules
IV. Interpersonal Communication
   A. Helpful communication
   B. Stressful communication
V. "Wearing" Your Workplace Attitude
   A. Service jobs
   B. Workplace attitude versus the "real you"
VI. Anger
   A. Maintaining control of feelings
   B. Dealing with angry people
VII. Time-Management Issues
   A. People work at different speeds
   B. Predictability and control
VIII. Dealing with People
   A. People-centered jobs and stress
   B. Burnout
IX. Attitudes Affect Job Stress
   A. Feelings about money, credit, debt
   B. Feeling resentment, jealousy, exploited
X. The Modern Workplace and Stress
   A. "Workshop Sources of Job Stress" handout
   B. How does your workplace measure up?
      1. Getting to work
      2. Work environment
      3. Office
      4. Plant

C. Video display terminals
    1. Eyestrain
    2. Fatigue and repetitive motion syndrome
    3. Radiation
    4. Back and shoulder pain
    5. Psychological stress
XI. Type-A Behavior Patterns
  A. General description
  B. Type-A personality and hostility
    1. Cynicism
    2. Hostile affect
    3. Aggressive response
    4. Health problems
  C. From Type A to Type B
    1. Type A and success
    2. Changing behavior patterns
XII. Conclusion
  A. "Suggestions for Dealing with Job Stress" handout
  B. Finding creative solutions to stress in the workplace

Workplace Stress

Handout

Why Do You Work?

Most of us spend at least 40 hours of every 168-hour week working. Although money is the primary motivator for most of us, we all have other reasons for working. Note the items that help explain why you work.

➤ Self-esteem: Your work makes you feel good about yourself—who you are, what you have accomplished.

➤ Feeling useful: Your work makes you feel good because you believe you are doing something beneficial for society.

➤ Helping: Your work involves helping other people.

➤ Recognition: Others know and appreciate what you do.

➤ Power: Your work enables you to control others.

➤ Independence: Your work enables you to control your own destiny.

➤ Fun: Your work is fun.

➤ Accomplishment: Your work permits you to take credit for having finished or built something of value.

➤ Self-exploration: Your work allows you to learn more about yourself and the world.

➤ Avoiding guilt: If you did not work, you would feel bad about yourself.

➤ Stimulation: Your work offers a chance to meet interesting people or do interesting things.

➤ Approval from others: You work to make family members and others happy and to keep them from criticizing you.

Handout

What's Stressful about Work?

	Best place I ever worked	Worst place I ever worked
The people:		
The work itself:		
The workplace:		
Attitudes:		

Workplace Stress

Handout

Workplace Sources of Job Stress

People are probably the most important source of job stress. However, the workplace itself can also be a factor. Having to work in a noisy, dirty, and uncomfortable environment can add significantly to your stress level. Go through this list and rate each item along a continuum from less stressful to more stressful.

Getting to work:
Commuting   Easy ——————————————— Hard

Parking   Easy ——————————————— Hard

Work environment:
Air quality   Fresh ——————————————— Stale/recirculated
                   Clean ——————————————— Dusty/smelly

Heat and air
conditioning   Comfortable ————————————— Uncomfortable

Lighting   Good ——————————————— Poor

Work space   Clean ——————————————— Dirty
                   Comfortable ————————————— Uncomfortable
                   Private ——————————————— Not private

Restrooms   Clean ——————————————— Dirty

Break room   Clean ——————————————— Dirty

Office:
Noise   Quiet ——————————————— Noisy

Desk supplies   New/usable ———————————— Broken/nonexistent

Workshop 2

Telephone	Reliable ———————————	Unreliable
Ringer/pager	Quiet ———————————	Noisy
Copier	Reliable ———————————	Unreliable
	Quiet ———————————	Noisy
Fax	Reliable ———————————	Unreliable
Typewriter	Reliable ———————————	Unreliable
Computer	Reliable ———————————	Unreliable
Printer	Quiet ———————————	Noisy

Plant:
Noise	Quiet ———————————	Noisy
Machinery	Reliable ———————————	Unreliable
Maintenance	Regular ———————————	Only when broke
	Professional ———————————	Nonprofessional
	Safety oriented ———————————	Shortcuts allowed
Work areas	Clean ———————————	Dirty
	Safe ———————————	Hazardous
Storage	Neat ———————————	Disorganized
Vehicles:	Reliable ———————————	Unreliable

Workplace Stress

Handout

Dealing with Job Stress

Identify sources of job stress:
1. _____
2. _____
3. _____
4. _____
5. _____
6. _____
7. _____
8. _____
9. _____
10. _____
11. _____
12. _____

Identify stressor patterns:
_____
_____
_____
_____

If you do nothing, what will likely happen? _____
_____
_____
_____
_____
_____
_____
_____
_____
_____
_____

Solutions (if you decide to act):
   S = Simple solution to make less stressful.
   C = More complicated; requires some cooperation from employer/co-workers.
   M = Major changes required to resolve very stressful situations.

Stressors 1–12	Solutions (S, C, M)	Plan of attack

Workplace Stress

Handout

Evaluation Form

This workshop offers participants an opportunity to examine stress in the workplace. It covers some of the most common stressors found on the job and looks at the stress problems faced by people with Type-A personalities.

Learning Objectives:
► To help participants understand the relationship among various sources of stress in the workplace.
► To explain research findings regarding the Type-A behavior personality.
► To explore options for dealing with job stress.

Please respond to these questions by circling the answers you agree with. Your comments will be used to help improve future programs.

1. The presenter fulfilled my expectations of what I wanted to learn from this workshop.

    Very much   Pretty much   Somewhat   Not at all

    Comments: _____
    _____
    _____
    _____

2. I can use the information I obtained in this workshop in my job and/or personal relations.

    Very much   Pretty much   Somewhat   Not at all

    Comments: _____
    _____
    _____
    _____

Workshop 2

3. The presenter knew the material, was organized, and presented the information clearly.

   Very much   Pretty much   Somewhat   Not at all

   Comments: _____
   _____
   _____
   _____

4. What would you have liked the presenter to do differently?
   _____
   _____
   _____
   _____

5. What did you like most about this workshop?
   _____
   _____
   _____
   _____

Workshop 3

➤ Understanding Anger

Learning Objectives
- ➤ To help participants understand that anger is a normal response in certain situations.
- ➤ To demonstrate how feeling angry affects people.

Introduction

Anger is one of the most stressful emotions a person experiences. In this workshop, we talk about where anger comes from, why people are so reluctant to deal with it, how anger creates stress in our lives, and some things an angry person might want to consider before deciding to act.

This workshop includes exercises that will help participants become more comfortable with discussing their anger. Because anger is a serious and broad topic, it is a good idea, especially if little time is available, to approach this material simply, factually, and with a sense of humor. The instructor's goal should be to offer participants a guide for dealing with their anger, not to rectify past injustices or cure psychological dysfunctions. Workshop participants who discover that they have a lot of unresolved anger should be referred to counseling. (For a complete series of workshops on anger, refer to Family Service America's Family Life Education Workshop Model, *Anger*.[1])

Handouts
- ➤ Workshop Outline

Workplace Stress

> ➤ What Messages Did You Receive about Anger When You Were Growing Up?
> ➤ Value Systems
> ➤ Factors to Consider before Expressing Anger
> ➤ What Do You Hope to Gain?
> ➤ Evaluation Form

Why People Are Afraid of Anger

Anger is frightening. People are afraid of their feelings of anger and of having to deal with angry people. Talking about anger can have a strong emotional impact on you if you've never dealt with these feelings before. The primary goal of this workshop is to make anger less scary for you—to help you see that anger is a normal response in certain situations.

People don't like to come right out and say, "I'm angry," so they try to find some other expression (a euphemism) to describe how they feel. There are many different ways to describe anger in English.

You might want to ask participants to share with the group expressions they use when they are angry. Record these on a flip chart, overhead, or chalkboard. Try to get one or two contributions from each participant. Some of the answers may be vulgar or slang. If the instructor or participants are offended by the language, ask them to "keep it clean" and use abbreviations or initials on the large list. For example, substitute "P.O.'d" for "pissed off." Refer to the handout for euphemisms people use instead of saying they are angry. The following lists just a few expressions people use to indicate that someone is angry.

Fury, indignation, irate, mad, dander, dudgeon, in a pet, huffy, P.O.'d, in a fit of pique, temper, annoyed, exasperated, infuriated, irritated, enraged, incensed, steamed up, taking umbrage, irked, vexed, aggravated, seeing red, losing one's temper, sore, in a snit, ticked off, indignant, stung, cross, rankled, slow burn, blowing up, making a scene, beside oneself, livid, raising cain, tearing up the place, having a cat fit, raising the roof, having a hemorrhage, blowing one's stack, fit to be tied, mad as a wet hen, testy, grouchy, surly, fractious, cranky, honked off.

Most of us are afraid of anger because we have learned to associate anger with destructive and violent behavior. Many of us have received strong negative messages about anger. We've been taught that anger is bad, that people who act angry are:

➤ Crazy
➤ Mad
➤ Out of control

➤ Hysterical
➤ Immature
➤ Sinful
➤ Unladylike/not gentlemanly
➤ Uncivilized

Distribute the "What Messages Did You Receive about Anger When You Were Growing Up?" handout. Ask participants to write in their thoughts about these messages.

Can you remember what you were told about anger as a child? Were you warned against losing your temper or told not to make a scene or act crazy? Were you scolded for "getting hysterical" or "acting emotional"? Some adults carry painful memories of having been blamed or punished for being angry.

Children receive messages about anger by observing their parents and other adults in their lives. Adults who are not skilled at handling anger may fall into one of two categories: *anger stuffers* or *anger exploders*.

Anger stuffers are people who try not to let their anger show. They experience a "cold fury" that they control with silence. Anger stuffers try to hide their anger, but it's pretty obvious when they are angry. Their anger can last a long time.

Anger exploders express anger by shouting, or even becoming violent. Their anger is loud, active, and occasionally destructive, but it may dissipate within a short period.

Growing up with either of these extremes, a child learns to be afraid of anger. In some families, one parent is a stuffer and the other an exploder, a classic case of attraction of opposites. If the couple aren't able to work out a compromise to find an acceptable way to express anger within the family, a power struggle may ensue. Children growing up in this kind of situation learn to view anger as a constant state of friction and tension.

Children receive other messages about anger from adults. They may learn to throw a tantrum when they want something or to repress their anger if they want to please their parents and teachers. In some dysfunctional families, a child may learn that it's important to control emotions and avoid dealing with them.

Children also pick up adults' stereotypical attitudes toward anger. For example, we've all heard that redheads are quick-tempered. And some people allege that people of a particular ethnic group or region of the country are "hotheads."

Society's attitude toward the expression of anger in men is different from its attitute toward women's expression of anger. Is it more acceptable for a man to express his anger with aggressive behavior? Why are men perceived as being more prone to violence than are women?

All of these messages and misconceptions add to our fear of anger. Because anger is so frightening, people attempt to run away from their own and other people's anger rather than deal with it. Some people try to change the subject or deny the anger. Others may become defensive and accuse others of making them angry. Many people deny feeling angry, but admit to some other feeling, usually a euphemism that means the same thing as anger; for example, "I'm not angry, but I'm very disappointed."

It's important to understand that the behaviors we associate with anger are not the same as the feeling of anger. The behavioral part of anger is usually what scares us, but sometimes feeling angry can be a frightening experience. For example, feeling angry can be frightening

- If you seldom allow yourself to feel anger
- When your feeling of anger is much stronger than usual
- When being angry runs counter either to the way you see yourself—"I am not the kind of person who gets angry"—or to your beliefs and values
- When your anger makes you feel as though you are losing your self-control or "going crazy"

What's really scary about anger is that *you can't predict how a person will act when he or she gets angry.* You never know who will remain calm and thoughtful and who will pull out a gun and start shooting. In sum, unpredictability and the potential for violence make anger frightening.

Defining Anger

People feel angry when they feel attacked or threatened in some way. When you feel that you are being attacked either physically or psychologically, you experience what is called a stress response. Thus, feeling angry—attacked—is one kind of stress. People may experience a similar stress response with fear or if they become very upset about something.

There are different degrees of anger, of course—from mild irritation to extreme outrage. When your anger makes you feel that you can't tolerate the very existence of a person, thing, or idea, then anger turns into hate. And when anger is stored up over time, it turns into resentment. Regardless of how you describe your feeling, the root cause is still anger!

Where Does Anger Come From?

Anger is a normal response to feeling threatened or attacked. It is a feeling, neither "good" nor "bad." When we get angry, we respond in two ways:

1. First, our body goes through the physiological changes associated with stress. That is, we feel threatened or attacked, and our body gets ready to do something about it.

2. Second, we do something in response to these feelings. This part, our behavioral response, is what scares people about anger because it is unpredictable and potentially violent or destructive.

What Makes You Angry?

The anger response begins with the perception of a threat or attack. If you don't perceive something as a threat or attack, you won't get angry.

Ask participants to share things or situations that make them angry. Record their responses and use these examples to show how the feeling of anger may be an appropriate response when one feels attacked or threatened. Pick out a key word or phrase from each response and write it on a flip chart, chalkboard, or overhead. Save this list; it may be useful later to show how anger can be triggered by an attack on one's value system or sources of self-esteem.

Threats and Attacks That Set Off Your "Anger Alarm"

Distribute the "Value Systems" handout.

There are important differences between attacks on who you are and attacks on what you believe in. An attack on what you believe in is directed at your value system. Your value system

- Tells you the difference between right and wrong, good and bad
- Sets expectations regarding your behavior (and other people's behavior) and lets you know how things should be
- Defines your beliefs regarding fairness and justice

When you feel that your values are being violated, you get angry. For many people in our society, unfairness and injustice trigger a strong anger response. The more important something is to you, the more angry you will become if you sense that it is being violated. Because we all have different value systems, we don't all get angry over the same things.

A useful discussion exercise at this point is to ask participants the following questions.

- Why do we all have different value systems?
- Would we be better off if we all shared the same value system?
- What can you do when a person who is the source of your anger has a completely different value system and consequently does not understand why you are angry?

Attacks on *who you are* are directed at your sources of self-esteem. The terms *self-esteem* and *self-worth* describe how you value yourself. Self-esteem enables us to feel good about who and what we are and is usually tied into how well we are living up to our values.

Some people rely heavily on a single source of self-esteem, for example, making a lot of money or being beautiful. In such instances, self-esteem can be shaky and the individual may be more vulnerable to anger. If the person's source of self-esteem is threatened—for example, a man who values money highly loses his job or a woman for whom beauty means everything begins to age—trouble ensues.

Think about situations that make you angry. Do your values and sources of self-esteem make you more vulnerable to anger? What triggers your anger? Look at the list of things that make you angry that you wrote down earlier. Can you see how each represents an attack on your value system or sources of self-esteem?

Your value system is being attacked when you believe that:
- People should do or be something (e.g., be considerate, play fair, be honest, etc.)
- People should not do or be something (e.g., be rude, lie, manipulate others, etc.)
- An injustice has been done

Your self-esteem is being threatened when you feel that someone
- Treats your feelings as unimportant or irrelevant
- Shows no respect for you
- Demeans or abuses you
- Belittles something in which you take pride

The following are some general examples of anger-provoking situations. (The instructor may wish to use more specific examples.)
- Perception of unfair treatment or prejudice
- Unfulfilled expectations
- Other people failing to live up to what you believe is right
- Being treated as a less-than-competent adult (like a child)

Your relationship to the source of your anger may affect your anger response. When you perceive that the other person is "superior" to you in knowledge or experience, what he or she says may hurt you more. Conversely, criticism from a younger, less experienced person is easier to take because you may feel that this person is "inferior" to you, less skilled, or not as well informed. One technique that may be helpful in coping with anger is to consider the source and attempt to *discount* it.

What Can You Do about Your Anger?

The stress-response aspect of anger is involuntary. However, you can learn to live with the stress or find ways to make the situation less stressful.

If your current way of dealing with anger works for you, then you have no problem. But if you find that your anger adds a lot of stress to your life, then you might want to consider some alternatives. Try accepting your anger as a normal reaction and stop feeling bad or guilty when you get angry. Learn to cope with the stress of anger first, then decide how to act.

Holding It In or Letting It Out?

What are your choices when you get angry? You can hold your anger in (like the "anger stuffers" discussed earlier) or find some way to let it out.

It's not always a bad idea to repress your anger. In fact, it may be a very smart thing to do if you are in danger of being harmed. On the other hand, if you are the type of person who regrets not having stood up for yourself, holding your anger in may hurt your self-esteem, which can be very stressful.

Distribute the "Factors to Consider before Expressing Anger" handout. Ask participants to follow along.

Assuming that you have taken time to cool down, considered other options, yet still feel a need to express your anger, ask yourself what you hope to accomplish. Here are some things to consider:

- Will telling the person who made you angry how you feel add to your self-esteem?
- Will expressing yourself satisfy your need for justice?
- Will it lower the level of stress in your life?
- What will happen if you get nothing for your trouble?
- How will you feel if the other person "shoots you down"?

Expressing anger is a risky business. People may not accept your anger. It's possible that you may get hurt if you decide to share your feelings with others. It's important to think carefully and to have some goals in mind before expressing your anger to someone.

Distribute copies of the "What Do You Hope to Gain?" handout and ask workshop participants to follow along.

Ask yourself what you expect from the other person. The handout describes four levels of response, each of which is more difficult to obtain from someone who has made you angry.

- At the very least, you would hope to obtain *validation*. ("Oh, you're angry.")
- With luck, you might get a *sincere apology*. ("Oh, you're angry. I'm sorry I made you feel that way!")
- Even better than a sincere apology is the person's *promise to fix what's wrong*. (I"m sorry I made you angry. I'll try to patch things up.")
- And the very best response is a *promise to change future behavior*. (You're angry and I'm really sorry I made you feel that way. I'll try to fix what I did wrong and I won't do it again.")

It takes a mature person to promise to fix what's wrong and it takes wisdom and sensitivity to promise to change future behavior. If you are fortunate, you might be able to get validation and a sincere apology from your children. If you can get all four responses from anyone, you are indeed a lucky person. And if you can get all four responses from a lover or spouse, you have a good chance of maintaining a successful relationship over a long period.

Negotiating Anger

To confront the source of your anger is to start a process of negotiation. To negotiate you must give something in order to get something, which may strike you as being unfair in that you're the one who's angry. Fairness aside, many people are unwilling to give anything unless they get something in return.

When you negotiate, the less you ask for, the more likely you are to get it. The easier you make it for the other person to comply with your request, the more likely they are to do so.

Be reasonable in determining what is possible and what makes sense in a given situation with a particular person. Don't ask for something the other person can't give. Reasonableness also means being specific when explaining your expectations. Make your request as reasonable, specific, and as "doable" as possible.

Before you negotiate, decide what you are willing to give up in order to get what you want. Set priorities—some things may be more negotiable than others. Because your goal is to get the other person to invest in a solution to a problem, think about incentives that you might offer to get that investment. An important incentive might be your agreeing to stop being angry.

Conclusion

We began by looking at why anger frightens people. People are afraid of anger for many different reasons and many people will try to escape when faced with an angry person.

We learned that anger is primarily a stress response that occurs when your self-esteem or values are threatened or attacked.

We also discussed what you can do about your anger—whether you should hold it in or let it out. Many of us lack skills for dealing with anger. Hopefully, we can pass along what we've learned here to our children so that they will be better able to deal with anger.

References

1. Steven B. Zwickel, *Anger* (Milwaukee: Family Service America, Inc., 1992).

Handout

Outline for Workshop 3

I. Introduction
II. Why People Are Afraid of Anger
    A. Euphemisms for describing anger
    B. Associating anger with destructive/violent behavior
    C. Messages we receive about anger
        1. Anger stuffers
        2. Anger exploders
    D. Expressions of anger in men and women
    E. Behavior versus feeling
III. Defining Anger
    A. Where does anger come from?
    B. What makes you angry?
    C. Anger alarm
        1. Threats to your value system
        2. Threats to your self-esteem
IV. What Can You Do about Your Anger?
    A. Holding anger in versus letting it out
    B. Considering your options
    C. Considering consequences of your behavior
    D. What do you hope to gain?
V. Negotiating Anger
    A. Confronting the source of your anger
    B. Reasonableness and compromise
VI. Conclusion

Workplace Stress

Handout

What Messages Did You Receive about Anger When You Were Growing Up?

Can you remember what you were told about anger as a child? Comments children hear about anger may stay with them for a long time. You may have been told that people who act angry are:
- Crazy
- Mad
- Out of control
- Hysterical
- Immature
- Sinful
- Unladylike/not gentlemanly
- Uncivilized

Or you may remember being warned against:
- Losing your temper
- Making a scene
- Getting hysterical or emotional
- Acting crazy

You may even have painful memories of being blamed or punished for becoming angry. What messages did you receive about anger when you were growing up?

_____
_____
_____
_____
_____
_____
_____
_____
_____
_____
_____
_____
_____

Handout

Value Systems

Children internalize the messages they receive from adults. Adults give us our system of values, the things we believe in. From this value system, we learn to tell the difference between:
- Right and wrong
- Good and evil
- Appropriate and inappropriate behavior

Our value systems also determine what we expect from ourselves and others. Our value systems may include a need to believe in fairness and justice in the world, the belief that the wicked will be punished and the righteous will be rewarded. Such beliefs are not logical, but they are necessary for us to function as civilized human beings:
- To help us explain random events
- To justify being "good"

Workplace Stress

Handout

Factors to Consider before Expressing Anger

The following are some things to think about before you express your anger:
- What are the chances of your being physically harmed or killed?
- Are you ready to risk ending a relationship?
- Is there the possibility that you will lose your job, career, status, or honor?

Consider practical issues before expressing your anger:
- When is the best time to do it?
- Where is the best place to do it?
- Will other people be around or will you be able to express yourself in private?
- Are you prepared to deal with other issues that might come up if you express your anger?
- Have you considered carefully what you hope to gain by expressing your anger?

Should you decide to express your anger, and assuming that you have taken some time to cool down and consider other options, what do you hope to accomplish?
- Will expressing your anger increase your self-esteem?
- Will it satisfy your need for justice?
- Will it lower the level of stress in your life?
- What will happen if you get nothing for your trouble?
- How will you feel if the other person "shoots you down"?

Handout

What Do You Hope to Gain?

Expressing anger can be risky because you never know how other people will react to your telling them that you're angry. Before confronting someone who has provoked you, it's a good idea to have some goals in mind. Think about what kind of response you would like to obtain. What do you expect from the other person? The following describes four levels of response, each of which is progressively more difficult to obtain from someone who has made you angry:

1. At the very least, you would hope to get "Oh, you're angry."
2. With luck you might get "Oh, you're angry. I'm sorry I made you feel that way!"
3. Even better than that is "I'm sorry I made you angry. I'll try to patch things up."
4. And the very best response is "You're angry and I'm really sorry I made you feel that way. I'll try to fix what I did and I won't do it again."

It takes a mature person to give response 3 and it requires wisdom and sensitivity to give response 4.
- ➤ If you are a fortunate parent, you might be able to get responses 1 and 2 from your children.
- ➤ If you get all four responses from anyone, you are indeed a lucky person.
- ➤ If you get all four responses from a lover or spouse, you have a good chance of maintaining a successful relationship over a long period.

Workplace Stress

Handout

Evaluation Form

Anger is one of the most stressful emotions a person experiences. This mini-workshop looked at where anger comes from, why people are reluctant to deal with it, how anger adds to the level of stress in our lives, and some things an angry person might consider before deciding to act on his or her anger.

Learning Objectives:
- ➤ To help participants understand that anger is a normal response in certain situations.
- ➤ To explore some of the reasons why people are so afraid of anger.
- ➤ To discuss different ways to deal with anger.

Please respond to these questions by circling the answers you agree with. Your comments will be used to help improve future programs.

1. The presenter fulfilled my expectations of what I wanted to learn from this workshop.

    Very much   Pretty much   Somewhat   Not at all

    Comments: _____
    _____
    _____
    _____

2. I can use the information I obtained in this workshop in my job and/or personal relations.

    Very much   Pretty much   Somewhat   Not at all

    Comments: _____
    _____
    _____
    _____

Workshop 3

3. The presenter knew the material, was organized, and presented the information clearly.

   Very much   Pretty much   Somewhat   Not at all

   Comments: _____
   _____
   _____
   _____

4. What would you have liked the presenter to do differently?
   _____
   _____
   _____
   _____

5. What did you like most about this workshop?
   _____
   _____
   _____
   _____

Workshop 4

➤ Anger in the Workplace

Learning Objectives

- ➤ To understand where anger in the workplace comes from.
- ➤ To see how anger is often expressed in sneaky anger games.
- ➤ To consider ways to reduce anger and game playing in the workplace.

Introduction

This workshop is the second of two mini-workshops on anger. The first workshop introduced the idea that anger is a normal response to threatening situations and that most of us have a choice of responses when we get angry. This workshop focuses on how anger applies to work settings. We will examine some of the sources of anger in the workplace and share strategies.

Handouts

- ➤ Workshop Outline
- ➤ Where Does Anger in the Workplace Come From?
- ➤ Sneaky Anger Games in the Workplace
- ➤ Reducing Anger in the Workplace
- ➤ Evaluation Form

Why Talk about Anger in the Workplace?

As a warm-up exercise, distribute the "Where Does Anger in the Workplace Come From?" handout. Ask participants to check off the items that apply to their workplaces and to consider what about these items makes them angry. Ask whether they can see a pattern of anger-producing behaviors.

Workplace Stress

After reviewing the learning objectives for this workshop, the instructor may wish to summarize points covered in workshop 3, "Understanding Anger."

- People are often afraid of anger because (1) they have received many negative messages about anger while growing up, and (2) anger is closely associated with unpredictable, violent, and destructive behavior.
- Anger is a normal response to feeling threatened or attacked. Usually, it is triggered by an attack on your *self-esteem* (who you are) or *value system* (what you believe in).
- Although anger creates an involuntary stress response, you do have choices. When you feel angry, you can choose your behavioral reactions. You can decide to hold your anger in or express it.
- Trying to hold your anger in can be very stressful, and you may not succeed. Your anger may eventually be expressed in sneaky anger games.
- If you decide to confront the source of your anger, you are able to decide when, where, and how this will occur. You may have to *negotiate*, that is, give something in order to get something from the person or persons who have made you angry.

To succeed in the workplace you must exercise self-control. Anger and other strong emotions are generally not acceptable. But controlling your anger can be extremely stressful and affect your sense of self-worth. What, then, can you do with your anger when you are unable to express it directly?

Sources of Anger in the Workplace

Surrendering Control over Your Life

Working for a living almost always requires you to surrender some control over your life. Outside the workplace, you may make the decisions, but in the workplace, you must follow orders and policies that you may not understand or agree with. You may feel like a cog in a great machine, unable to change or influence the system. You may feel that:

- You have no say in decisions that are made.
- Your dress, behavior, hours, and even where you will live (relocation) are determined by others.
- You (and your family) are at the mercy of the economic system (recessions, layoffs, inflation, and bankruptcies).
- You have no place to take your complaints (at least, where they will be listened to).
- "Whistle-blowing" is risky. Complainers often suffer severe retribution.

Depending on where you work, "fitting in" may be defined as actively demonstrating enthusiasm for your employer—being a "company booster."

You may be expected to sacrifice time with family and friends for your career and to put your own needs and personal life last. The organization's culture may demand that you give up part of your own identity and culture. Some people welcome the opportunity to become part of a large organization, but for those who cherish their individuality, conforming can be painful.

Playing by Someone Else's Rules

In the workplace, a person's self-esteem is very exposed and vulnerable. We are judged on the quality and speed of our work. If the product of our labor isn't up to standard, our deficiencies are noticed and criticized, while our good qualities may be ignored.

In addition, we may have to "make do" with the tools we are given, no matter how obsolete or cumbersome they are. We learn to work on outdated equipment, to shout into substandard telephones, or bring our own pencil sharpener to work. We put up with these annoyances "because that's the way we do it here," even if it defies logic.

Today, few, if any, people in the United States would allow someone to arrange their marriage. However, if we want a job badly enough, we'll agree to work with the devil himself. For the most part, we accept our work assignments with few complaints. We want to be thought of as "team players"; we want to please the boss. We sit under a drafty vent or next to a noisy computer printer, struggling valiantly to get along with these "strangers" 40 hours a week.

Unless you operate your own business, your influence in the workplace is limited. You have no say over whom you must work with, and regardless of how rude customers are, you can't hang up on them. This inability to affect your environment leads to feelings of helplessness, anger, and perhaps depression and early burnout.

Adapting to Others' Values

There isn't a lot of give and take in the workplace—you either adapt to other peoples' values or you don't work. When conflict develops between the employer's values and workers' values, the "good guys" don't always win.

Sometimes it seems like everyone but the few people at the very top of the heap are forced to adapt to other people's needs. Sellers adapt to buyers, borrowers try to please lenders, and everybody tries to appease the I.R.S.

To survive in the work world, you need to get along—and go along—with others. You need to learn to please the boss, the customers, the shareholders, and/or the accountants. To survive, you must be a *team player* and put your own needs last.

Masking Your Feelings

In the past two decades, the United States has become more of a service economy. Because more and more people are involved in selling services, there is a growing emphasis on providing good service and to *always be nice.*

More people today are getting paid for "emotional labor." People who are good at emotional labor are able to "manage their feelings to create a publicly observable facial and body display consistent with the image required by their employers."[1] In other words, they are good at acting the way a bank teller, receptionist, flight attendant, maitre d', or bill collector is supposed to act.

➤ What happens to people whose jobs require them to be "nice" all the time?
➤ How must it feel to put a grin on your face every morning, then keep it there for eight hours?
➤ What can people do when something or someone at work makes them angry? Arlie Hochschild says that wearing a phony smile all day at work has a detrimental effect on a person's life.[2]
➤ Some workers buy wholeheartedly into the forced cheerfulness. These workers perceive their smiles as being real. They don't think they are acting and aren't aware that they are wearing a mask. However, such workers, who comply completely with company guidelines for managing emotions, often experience severe stress, suffer from burnout, become numb to and out of touch with their real feelings, and may eventually lose track of that which is authentic and real in their life.
➤ For others, wearing a smile and putting on a cheerful attitude are part of dressing for the job. They want to project the right attitude and are concerned lest they fail to show appropriate spirit. They worry a lot about whether others perceive them as insincere.
➤ Still others view acting as just part of the job. They understand that the role they play at work is not who they are. They compartmentalize the different parts of the their lives and don't permit the stresses of work to carry over into their personal lives (or vice versa).

People lose control over their emotional life when their employer dictates how they should act and pretend to feel. Such policies can leave workers feeling helpless and unable to influence or control their life. As a result such workers feel helpless rage over their loss of individuality.

Unfairness of the Work World

Despite all of the laws passed against discrimination, promoting fair competition, and requiring equal treatment, we still can't seem to change some of the basic injustices in the workplace. Time and again we find that hiring, promotion, and success are unrelated to an individual's merits. People still get or don't get jobs, promotions, and contracts because of their:

➤ Looks: The fat, the disfigured, the "funny-looking" people don't get the nod.
➤ Race, religion, ethnic origin: Discrimination is illegal but it still happens every day. Discrimination is very hard to prove, and complaining can give you the reputation of being a troublemaker.
➤ Age: Try to get a job after you reach middle age; no wonder the market for men's cosmetics is booming!
➤ Sex: Many employers still have a double standard. "Women's" jobs are still different from "men's" jobs, and women earn only about two-thirds of what men do.
➤ Contacts: In many places, it's who you know that counts.
➤ Seniority: Stick it out long enough and you rise to the top, regardless of whether you know what you're doing or not.
➤ Playing office politics: Often, it's better to be good at brown-nosing and back-stabbing than at doing your job.
➤ Ability to play third base: In an episode of the TV show "Cheers," ex-major leaguer Sam Malone wins a promotion because the company team needs a pitcher. It happens in real life, too.

It's very difficult to prove bias and discrimination in a court of law. Lawyers can always find some "legitimate" reason why so-and-so got the job/promotion/contract. Those who are least qualified for the job but able to manipulate people are often the most successful in the workplace.

Most of us are pragmatic and understand that injustices occur. We compensate by learning to play the "employment game." For persons who can't discern the rules of this game, the work world can seem unreal. They never quite figure out why they can't get ahead and experience frustration and rage when they don't. Some keep on trying, fighting the injustices they see around them. Others give up and become part of the permanently unemployable—condemned by society for their "bad attitude" and their inability or unwillingness to conform.

In *Something Happened*, novelist Joseph Heller writes about the fear that rules the corporate workplace. Everyone is afraid of everyone else—a fear born of jealousy, envy, and resentment. The organizational hierarchy breeds anger, which periodically erupts into sabotage, labor troubles, and management burnout.

Most American workers long for some control over their work.[3] They aren't lazy or unmotivated, nor do they need an iron fist to get them to work hard. What they want is some input into how things are done. They want to be taken seriously by higher-ups.

Robert Townsend argues that most people want more than money from their work. People will work harder if their work rewards and satisfies their

Workplace Stress

egos and meets other personal needs. Townsend believes that we must "humanize" the work environment so that people obtain more control over this major part of their lives.

Games People Play in the Workplace

In the workplace, where expressing anger is usually not acceptable, people may play psychological games.[4] Such games allow people to strike at the source of their anger in such a way that they can avoid taking responsibility for becoming angry and make retaliation impossible.

Psychological games are *role-playing* games, whereby you take on certain characteristics and follow specific rules. People involved in such games take turns and even keep score, just as though they were playing a board game. In sneaky anger games, a player's goal is to get a need met. The payoff for winning may be the opportunity to control, hurt, or humiliate someone else or it may be just a safe way to express strong feelings. When playing such games, it's important not to get caught playing—to always deny that you are angry or that you are trying to hurt another player.

Before distributing and going through the "Sneaky Anger Games in the Workplace" handout, make sure participants understand that people play games because they have no other way of getting their feelings out. Workshop participants who recognize themselves as having played some of the games described in the handout may need some reassurance that this doesn't mean that they are bad people; it simply means that they had no other tools available with which to deal with their anger. Other participants may indicate that they are currently involved in an ongoing game and ask for help in quitting. Explain that the only way to stop playing a psychological game is to stop playing. Ending a long-standing game involves the risk of ending the relationship, even a love relationship. (A couple might have to work out such issues in marriage counseling or psychotherapy.) In the workplace, deciding to stop playing a game might make things better or it could result in being fired.

Sneaky Anger Games

The following are some examples of anger games that people play. In these games, people get their anger out without actually having to admit that they are angry.

Collusion

In this game, the more a player helps you do something, the worse things get. Collusion often starts with "Here, let me help you," and ends with "But, I was only trying to help!" This game can be very aggressive if you attack people when and where they are most vulnerable. For example,

- Offering someone on a diet a fattening dessert
- Doing such a bad job helping out on a project that it has to be redone
- Asking a compulsive spender to go shopping with you for "just a few little things"

Chronic Sickness

Some people use their illnesses and injuries to gain more than just sympathy. A person who plays the chronic sickness game tries to get you to do a job or take on a responsibility, claiming that he or she is "not up to it." Usually, this game involves chronic medical problems—conditions that the player has had for a while. People who play this game may use physical ailments, mental disorders, or drug and alcohol problems as their bargaining chips. The player wins this game when others are forced to do his or her job. Chronic sickness players control others by demanding special consideration. For example,

- A co-worker can't help out with inventory because of "doctor's orders."
- He or she claims to be unable to carry or lift things because of a "bad back" and insists that other people do the heavy lifting.
- People "tiptoe" around the person because they don't want to aggravate his or her "condition."

Chronic Forgetfulness

Everyone forgets things from time to time. A chronic forgetter, however, constantly forgets things that are important to you. For example, you will be told that something has been taken care of; then, after you have been lulled into a false sense of security, the forgetter lets you down hard!

Chronic Misunderstanding

This game is similar to chronic forgetfulness. You may think it's safe to rely on someone's memory, judgment, or common sense only to find that the person has misunderstood the most obvious directions. Endless memos and meetings are often the result of this game. You may find yourself having to explain the same things over and over (and feeling pretty dumb about it!). For example,

- Someone makes big plans for a company luncheon, then forgets to make the reservations.
- You relied upon someone to send out a business letter or announcement, but he or she leaves out an important item (date, time, place, or price).

Chronic Nonlearner

Perhaps you have been in a situation in which you have had to repeat the same instructions over and over because the person never quite seems

to "catch on." In the workplace, this game may go on until you decide to do what needs to be done yourself. You may feel stupid and incompetent for not being able to give clear directions. Part of the payoff for people who play this game is that they can criticize you for being too fussy, picky, or petty. For example, the chronic learner might say
> "I didn't realize that a monthly report is supposed to be sent out every month"
> "It's all your fault for forgetting to mention _____."

Time Warrior

These people use time as a weapon by playing two games, chronic lateness and procrastination, both of which can easily drive you to tears. These are the people who hold things up so that you have to scramble to make up for lost time. (Their payoff comes when your work looks rushed compared with theirs!) These people are controlling and frustrating, especially when out of sheer frustration you decide to do the job yourself. When you confront someone who is chronically late or a procrastinator, they always have an airtight excuse for why things didn't happen on time and it's *never* their fault. Examples include:
> A report you need to complete a job is late. When you finally get the report, you rush your work to catch up.
> The person in charge of the slide projector shows up late, forcing other presenters to improvise and appear to be poorly prepared.

Helpful Generalizer

People who play this game always claim that they were only doing what you said you wanted. In this game, your likes and dislikes are taken to be absolutes and everything you say is treated as though it were chiseled in stone. When you discover that your offhand comments and opinions are being taken seriously and interpreted as policy decisions, you feel extremely foolish and end up having to explain, apologize, etc. For example,
> Your assistant keeps ordering an expensive brand of floppy disks because the person who installed the computer used that brand.
> Your offhand comment that "someone ought to look into" something results in a long, detailed, superfluous report.

Holier-than-Thou

If you deal with someone who plays this game, prepare to be told over and over that you are wrong about everything. All of the motivational books, tapes, and seminars published in recent years have led to an increase in the number of smug, self-satisfied people who believe that they have found "the answer." Holier-than-thou people put you down and dis-

count you for not being privy to their special insights. These are the people who sadly shake their head and inform you that it's a shame you haven't
- Been through a motivational workshop
- Studied some ancient philosophy
- Read up on a new marketing technique
- Gone through years of psychoanalysis

Intellectualizer

These people know many theories but have little insight. You may be impressed by their knowledge while astounded by their inability to express their feelings. Intellectualizers don't take responsibility for their expressions of anger because they see themselves as being completely rational. They value reason and logic above all else. They like to tell you that you're "too emotional" and that you "don't make sense." For example, an intellectualizer is
- The person who explains why a rational, logical, mature person (like the intellectualizer) never gets angry
- The person who characterizes *your* expressions of anger as hysterical, psychotic, overemotional, etc.

Nonrewarder

Some people never say "thank-you" or "nice job!" These game players give you just enough encouragement to keep you working for a compliment. Nonrewarders never give anyone positive feedback unless they are forced to do so. When a nonrewarder does pay you a compliment, he or she will qualify and discount it until it's worthless. For example,
- You are told that your work is acceptable, but the nonrewarder would like to see you working up to your potential.
- You reach your goal or exceed it and are told that more is expected from you.

Helpless Victim

Have you ever tried your best to help someone solve a problem but come away feeling stupid and incompetent? This game begins with your being asked to help with a problem. After you agree to help, you discover that nothing you say or suggest is any good. No matter what you suggest, the other person has already thought of it and can tell you why it won't work. The longer the game goes on, the more inadequate you feel.

People play this game for different reasons, not all of which have to do with anger. Some want to convince themselves (and you) that they have exhausted all the possible alternatives and the problem is truly unsolvable. Others seek to confirm their belief that they are being unfairly victim-

Workplace Stress

ized by people and are therefore deserving of sympathy. For example,
- All of your attempts to help are answered, "Yes, but . . . "
- The longer you talk, the more hopeless the situation seems to be.

Doubt-Inducer

The doubt-inducer plays a very hostile game designed to crush your hopes and dreams. People who play this game are experts at finding the cloud behind the silver lining. They often play the role of devil's advocate or the "voice of reason" to prevent changes they oppose. Let everyone develop enthusiasm over a new idea or project and the doubt-inducer will offer facts and opinions to show that it won't work. With a few well-chosen words and comments, the doubt-inducer kills everyone's enthusiasm. Often, this person plays a verbal version of "collusion" (described above). For example, the person who waits for enthusiasm to peak, then offers a few "helpful observations" proving that something won't work or can't be done.

Remind participants that many other anger games people play involve money, sex, time, and guilt. The goal of these games is to find a way to express anger without admitting feelings of anger.

How to Stop Playing Anger Games

There is only one way to stop playing a psychological game: *stop playing!* To stop playing a game requires you to change your attitudes and behavior. It means, for example, that you stop rushing to pick up the pieces or to save the day when you've been caught in a game of collusion or chronic lateness. It means insisting that others accept responsibility for their behavior, making expectations clear, and not accepting excuses. Implementing these changes in the workplace may require establishing new rules for accountability and spelling out consequences for failure and success.

These goals may be difficult to achieve. For instance, others may be content to keep playing these games. The decision by one person either to change the rules of that game or to stop playing a game often results in the other players' terminating that relationship. More simply stated, your decision to stop playing games in the workplace may end relationships and might even get you fired.

As a general rule, people don't want to deal with another person's anger if they can avoid it. Think twice before you decide to discuss your feelings of anger with someone at work. You may be better off demonstrating that their behavior or words has had a negative effect on your work than trying to get them to deal with your anger. Linguistics professor Suzette Haden Elgin is a strong proponent of this approach.[5] In *The Gentle Art of Verbal*

Self-Defense, she discusses practical ways to deal with anger in situations in which emotional expression is not considered appropriate.

Can You Change the Rules?

Before you decide to stop playing a game, consider the following questions:
- What does the game player get out of playing a particular game? The opportunity to let anger out? A way to manipulate people? A means of compensating for lack of knowledge, skills, or real authority?
- Can the players be honest about what they want?
- Can you suggest other ways in which players can get what they want without playing games? What words or signals can people give so others will know what they want?
- If you try to stop playing a game, how will you deal with pressures to continue playing?

If participants are curious about how these games apply in other situations, the instructor can use the following paragraph to answer questions about sneaky anger games and relationships.

If you are tired of being the victim of your spouse's sneaky anger games and decide to stop playing, you may very well wind up separated or divorced. People play these games because they have needs that they want the other person to fill. Competent marriage and couples counselors are extremely careful when helping a couple communicate more clearly because doing so may end a relationship as well as a game. If the counselor helps end a game without offering an alternative way for individuals to meet their needs, the relationship can fall apart.

Dealing with Anger at Work

People often feel helpless in the workplace. They have little power to effect changes and nothing they do seems to make things better. The penalties for being a troublemaker far outweigh any advantages they might gain from working for change. As a result, people become angry.

The following ideas may help you develop a plan to deal with your anger in the workplace.

Identify What You Are Feeling

Is it anger or could it be something else? Other feelings that are sometimes confused with anger include:
- Boredom—tired of the routine, lack of stimulation
- Burnout—emotional exhaustion, loss of enthusiasm, withdrawal
- Depression—feeling helpless, hopeless, sad, distressed

Identify What Is Making You Angry

Where is your anger coming from? Are you angry at one particular person, several people, or the "system"? The "Reducing Anger in the Workplace" handout may help you get in touch with the source of your anger. Are you angry because of someone's behavior, way of communicating, attitude, lack of skills, way of handling problems or emergencies?

Identify the Most Appropriate Way to Deal with Your Anger

Workplace behavior is governed by unwritten rules that may prohibit or permit you to act. You may value truth, candor, and honesty, but in the workplace, a higher value is placed on getting along with others, having the proper attitude, and showing respect for your superiors.

Identify Who "Owns" the Problem

Are you aware of how you come across to other people? Is it possible that they do not care for your sense of humor, your demeanor, your attitude, or taste in clothes? In other words, the real cause of your anger may be how others respond to you. If others perceive you as not fitting in, they will rarely come right out and tell you. An important part of almost any job is getting along with other people. It's up to you to tune in to what people are not saying aloud—to *manage yourself* so that you do fit in. Books and workshops are available to help people learn these skills—how to dress and act appropriately, how to speak and write better, how to handle yourself in awkward situations at work. Use the library, adult education classes, business seminars, friends and relatives who are skilled at self-management, to improve your image in the workplace.

A Square Peg in a Round Hole

If your expectations when you started work were unrealistic, you may now be frustrated and disappointed. Today, people commonly have had more than one career. If you are angry and uncomfortable with your job, consider switching to a different field. Again, use your resources to find out what's available. Schools and libraries have a lot of materials on the labor market, changing careers, retraining programs, acquiring new skills, and where you can go for help and guidance.

Conclusion

We began by looking at some of the root causes of anger in the workplace—lack of control, helplessness, the need to adapt to other people's values, masking your real feelings, the unfairness of the work world, and fear and intimidation. Then we examined some of the games people play when they are unable to express their anger directly: collusion, chronic sickness, forgetfulness, misunderstanding, chronic learner, time warrior, helpful generalizer, holier-than-thou, intellectualizer, nonrewarder, helpless victim, and doubt-inducer. Finally, we discussed ways to reduce game playing and anger in the workplace.

If we sincerely want to do something about anger in the workplace, we must begin by rethinking our assumptions about what motivates people to work and how workers are treated. Should work offer more intangible benefits along with cold cash as incentives? Can anything be done about the inequalities inherent in the workplace? We need people to lead and people to follow, so it's unrealistic to think that we can do away with hierarchy completely. It's important, though, that we keep working for justice and fair treatment for all.

Effecting changes in the workplace requires special leaders, that is, people who are willing to take risks while channeling co-workers' energy into new directions and treating colleagues as valued members of an organization.

References

1. Arlie Russell Hochschild, *The Managed Heart: Commercialization of Human Feeling* (Berkeley, CA: University of California Press, 1983), p. 7.
2. Ibid., p. 41.
3. Robert Townsend, *Up the Organization* (New York: Fawcett Crest, 1970), pp. 59–60.
4. G. R. Bach and Herb Goldberg, *Creative Aggression* (New York: Doubleday, 1974).
5. Suzette Haden Elgin, *The Gentle Art of Verbal Self-Defense* (New York: Dorset Press, 1980).

Workplace Stress

Handout

Outline for Workshop 4

I. Introduction
II. Why Talk about Anger in the Workplace?
    A. Fear of anger
    B. Attacks on your self-esteem or value system
    C. Confronting anger
    D. Controlling anger versus expressing anger
III. Sources of Anger in the Workplace
    A. Surrendering control over your life
    B. Playing by someone else's rules
    C. Adapting to others' values
    D. Masking your feelings
    E. Unfairness of the work world
IV. Sneaky Anger Games in the Workplace
    A. Collusion
    B. Chronic sickness
    C. Chronic forgetfulness
    D. Chronic misunderstanding
    E. Chronic nonlearner
    F. Time warrior
    G. Helpful generalizer
    H. Holier-than-thou
    I. Intellectualizer
    J. Nonrewarder
    K. Helpless victim
    L. Doubt-inducer
V. How to Stop Playing Anger Games
    A. Stop playing
    B. Changing your attitudes and behavior
    C. Changing the rules
VI. Dealing with Anger at Work
    A. Identify what you are feeling
    B. Identify what is making you angry
    C. Identify the most appropriate way to deal with your anger
    D. Identify who "owns" the problem
    E. Are you a square peg in a round hole?
VII. Conclusion

Handout

Where Does Anger in the Workplace Come From?

In the workplace, people often don't express their anger overtly. Check the items that apply to you.

____ I can't tell whether I'm doing a good job.

____ People don't understand how long it takes to get things done here.

____ Most of the people I deal with are trying to cheat me.

____ My job is undefined—I don't know what I'm supposed to be doing.

____ Lots of other people here get away with murder.

____ Nobody ever tells me anything.

____ I often get blamed for other people's mistakes.

____ Nobody listens to me.

____ Few of the people I deal with tell the truth.

____ People don't stay at this losy job for more than a few months, but the workers are always blamed for being lazy goof-offs.

____ No one here ever asks me my opinion—how I feel about things.

____ All I ever get from my boss are promises.

____ Everyone complains when I make a mistake, but no one has ever taken the time to show me how to do things right.

____ This place is a pigsty, but I'm the only one who seems to care.

____ They expect us to work miracles, but they don't want to pay for quality work.

____ The "Mickey Mouse" around here is unbelievable—you have to fill out a form for every little thing.

Workplace Stress

Handout

Sneaky Anger Games in the Workplace

The goal of these games is to express anger without admitting feelings of anger or accepting responsibility for your feelings.

Collusion: The more "help" you get, the worse things become.
➤ Offering misleading advice to someone, causing him or her to do twice as much work as is necessary.
➤ Doing such a bad job helping out on a project that it has to be redone.

Chronic Sickness: People use their illnesses and injuries to get you to do a job or take on a responsibility. They also control people by demanding special consideration.
➤ Can't help co-workers do physical inventory because of "doctor's orders."
➤ Having to "tiptoe" around a person because you don't want to aggravate the "condition."

Chronic Forgetfulness: The chronic forgetter constantly manages to forget things that are important to you.

Chronic Misunderstanding: Similar. You find yourself explaining the same things over and over (and feeling pretty dumb about it!).
➤ The person who makes big plans for a company luncheon, then forgets to make reservations.
➤ You rely upon someone to send out a business letter or announcement, but he or she leaves out an important item (date, time, place, or price).

Chronic Nonlearner: You repeat the same instructions over and over, but the person never seems to catch on.
➤ "I didn't realize that monthly report is supposed to be sent out *every* month."
➤ "It's all your fault for forgetting to mention _____."

Time Warrior: They play two games, *chronic lateness* and *procrastination.*
➤ A report you need to complete a job is late. When you finally get the report, you rush your work to catch up.
➤ A person in charge of the slide projector shows up late, causing other presenters to improvise and appear unprepared.

Helpful Generalizer: Expressions of likes and dislikes are taken as absolutes; everything you say is treated as though it were chiseled in stone.
- Your assistant insists on ordering an expensive brand of floppy disks because the person who installed the computer used that brand.
- Your offhand comment that "someone ought to look into" something results in a long, detailed, superfluous report.

Holier-than-Thou: Puts you down for not being privy to some special insights. These people sadly shake their head and inform you that it's a shame that you haven't:
- Been through a motivational workshop
- Studied some ancient philosophy
- Read up on a new marketing technique
- Gone through years of psychoanalysis

Intellectualizer: Intellectualizers don't take responsibility for their expressions of anger because they see themselves as being completely rational.
- Explains why a rational, logical person (like the intellectualizer) never gets angry.
- Characterizes your expressions of anger as hysterical, psychotic, or overemotional.

Nonrewarder: Never says "thank you" or "nice job!" but gives you just enough encouragement to keep you working for a compliment.
- You're told that although your work is acceptable, you're not working up to your potential.

Helpless Victim: Nothing you say or suggest will work.
- All of your attempts to help are answered, "Yes, but . . . ."
- The longer you talk, the more hopeless the situation seems to be.

Doubt-Inducer: Finds the cloud behind the silver lining.
- Ready to offer a few "helpful observations" why something can't be done.

Adapted from G. R. Bach and Herb Goldberg, *Creative Aggression: The Art of Assertive Living* (New York: Doubleday, 1974).

Handout

Reducing Anger in the Workplace

Use this handout to take a critical look at your workplace in order to find the sources of your anger. After you understand why you are angry, you can begin to consider your options for trying to change or minimize the aggravating situation.

How Job Performance Is Evaluated
Value is placed on:
- Speed
- Accuracy
- Ability to see more than one solution
- Doing things exactly according to company policy
- Creativity
- Socializing outside work
- Learning new tasks quickly
- Getting along with the boss
- Having the right attitude
- Writing and speaking skills
- Listening skills
- Number of deals closed/projects finished/units sold
- Meeting management's quotas
- Reliability
- Thoroughness
- Making deals while staying out of jail

Hiring/Promotion Practices
Based on:
- Merit
- Personal contacts
- Person's looks, age, sex, religion, race
- Personal whims of management
- There are no promotions or raises

How Tasks Are Assigned
Tasks are most often assigned by:
- Order in which they come in

- Random
- Workers' seniority
- Workers' specialty

Workers' Input on Policy/Procedures
- All policies are spelled out in detailed manuals
- No discussion—memo or newsletter announces decision
- Meetings held with people affected, options explored, decision made
- Decisions made by group consensus at regular staff meetings
- No formal policies—All decisions made on the spot, broadcast via grapevine
- Decisions avoided whenever possible; committees used to delay/put things off

Complaints
Workers' problems and complaints are usually handled by:
- Ignoring them
- Transfer, driving out, or firing complainers
- Transfer, driving out, or firing anyone complained about
- Calling in people affected, options explored, decision made
- Following the procedures spelled out in detailed manuals
- Referral to headquarters for decision or nonaction

Control over Workers' Emotional Life
Workers are required to:
- Conceal all emotions—positive and negative
- Conceal negative feelings
- Maintain "professional distance" at all times
- Conceal feelings, but allowed to blow off steam in private
- Conceal feelings, but allowed to blow off steam to supervisors/co-workers

Rewards
- Incentives include bonuses and perks
- Success leads to promotion
- Formal recognition of good work—bonuses, perks, awards
- Informal recognition of good work—thanks and congratulations
- No rewards ever given besides paycheck

Taboos

Unacceptable behaviors include:
- Talking about how much money someone makes
- Criticizing organizational goals (or not taking them seriously)
- Criticizing the CEO's project
- Discussing your private life
- Saying anything good about the competition
- Admitting that a job is boring

Handout

Evaluation Form

In this workshop, we examined sources of anger in the workplace and shared ideas for coping.

Learning Objectives:
➤ To understand where anger in the workplace comes from.
➤ To see how anger comes out in sneaky anger games.
➤ To consider ways to reduce anger and game playing in the workplace.

Please respond to these questions by circling the answers with which you agree. Your comments will be used to help improve future programs.

1. The presenter met my expectations for what I wanted to learn from this workshop.

    Very much   Pretty much   Somewhat   Not at all

    Comments:_____
    _____
    _____
    _____

2. I can use the information I obtained in this workshop in my job and/or personal relations.

    Very much   Pretty much   Somewhat   Not at all

    Comments:_____
    _____
    _____
    _____

3. The presenter knew the material, was organized, and presented the information clearly.

   Very much   Pretty much   Somewhat   Not at all

   Comments:_____
   _____
   _____
   _____

4. What would you have liked the presenter to do differently?
   _____
   _____
   _____
   _____

5. What did you like most about this workshop?
   _____
   _____
   _____
   _____

Workshop 5

➤ Making the Most of Your Time

Learning Objectives

- ➤ To demonstrate different ways of thinking about time, the value we place on time, and how rhythms and cycles affect us.
- ➤ To learn how to use planning and scheduling to become more protective of one's time and energy.
- ➤ To understand how people play psychological games with time.

Introduction

This workshop is the first of two on time and time management. In recent years, many seminars, articles, and books on time management have appeared that leave people feeling guilty and inadequate. Often, authors greatly oversimplify the problems faced by millions of people who need to find some way to balance their commitments to work, home, marriage, friends, and other interests.

This workshop is different in that it attempts to empower participants. The material concentrates on the various ways in which we think about time. It explores two problem areas: the errors people make in estimating how much time is needed to do something and games people play relating to time.

Handouts

- ➤ Workshop Outline
- ➤ Tips on Schedules and Calendars
- ➤ Games People Play with Your Time

- Samples of personal calendars and schedules (to be collected by the instructor)
- Bibliography
- Evaluation Form

Time Management—A Popular Topic

Time management is a popular topic. Numerous magazines publish time-management tips for managers, parents, teachers, busy executives, young upwardly mobile professionals, and teenagers. Bookstores and libraries are full of books with expert advice on how to work more efficiently, how to streamline your life and your workplace, and how to avoid those nasty "time-wasters" that allegedly keep people from making it to the top. Many of these books also tell you how to do *more* work, as if that were the problem!

Most, if not all, of these books and articles offer readers the following suggestions:
- Make a list of what you need to do
- Decide what's most important (determine your priorities)
- Do what needs to be done in order of importance

Advice like this is patronizing. Most of us have learned this scheme of things by the time we finished third grade. Repeating it makes people feel guilty and inadequate—we keep making lists and still don't have enough time.

In this workshop you won't be told what you already know. You won't be exhorted to get organized and you won't be made to feel lazy, incompetent, or guilty. Participants sign up for time-management programs because they feel overwhelmed, helpless, and exhausted. It's important that they leave feeling empowered so that they can be more assertive and protective of their time and energy, don't have to play games with their time, and can use the skills they acquire here to get more out of life.

Why is time such a problem for so many people? Why is it so difficult to manage our time? Why can't we coordinate our schedule with other people's? Why does there never seem to be enough time to do all the things we want and need to do?

In the first part of this workshop we will discuss how we think about time. Then we will examine more closely two problems people have with time:
- Errors in estimating the time needed to do something
- Anger games people play with regard to time

Concepts of Time

Time is a source of stress and interpersonal conflict. Various factors influence how people perceive time.

Your *age* makes a difference in how you experience time. Children are notoriously impatient. They desire instant gratification and have trouble with concepts such as "soon" and "later." Adults generally consider being able to delay gratification and the ability to plan ahead as signs of maturity. An adult who is unable to wait patiently or to make plans might be viewed as being emotionally immature.

Where you live also influences your view of time. People in different parts of the country view the pace of life differently. Life in big cities may seem overwhelming to someone from a rural area of the country. But even the hectic pace of life in an American city might seem slow to someone from Japan! Although Americans in general place high value on punctuality, in some parts of the world, it is considered extremely rude to show up early for an appointment.

There are also *unwritten rules* or tacit conventions regarding time in some places. In small towns, for example, people may feel pressured to do things at a particular time—laundry is done on Monday, Christmas lights and decorations are put up the weekend after Thanksgiving, and so forth. People who adhere to these local customs never give them a second thought, although outsiders may find them very strange.

Your *cultural or geographical background* may influence your concept of time. People from warmer climates often work at a less hurried pace. With the arrival of air conditioning, this relaxed pace is fast disappearing. However, people in many cultures still consider hurrying or rushing as inappropriate. In these cultures, patience and protocol are valued over speed.

A major influence on your concept of time is the way in which *your parents* handled time. Your personal style of managing time may be a reflection of what you learned as a child. Your style of handling time may represent a rejection of their style or it may mimic their way. Whatever your parents' attitudes toward time, your style is sure to be affected in some way.

Your *psychological state* also affects your perception of time. The old adage "time flies when you're having fun" has become a cliché because it reflects a common perception of reality. People also lose track of time when they're going through an emotional crisis. People who are susceptible to mood swings experience greater changes in the apparent passage of time. Some drugs can also alter our perceptions of time.

Value of Time

In our society, time has a monetary value. In fact, some people value their time more than their money. When we purchase services, we put a monetary value on a person's time and may disregard the actual energy and expertise involved in performing a job. For example, hourly wages are often related to what we believe a day's pay should be. Professionals often bill clients for their time, not the job. Thus, a brief visit to a physician costs less than a full examination.

In the business world, the saying "time is money" has become a cliché. Many American businesses and organizations are adopting new corporate philosophies based on the quality-management methods pioneered by W. Edwards Deming, Philip Crosby, and Joseph Juran. An aspect of quality management is the "just-in-time" concept, whereby inventory is moved quickly in order to reduce the cost of storage (usually based on how long items remain in a warehouse). And if our lives weren't hectic enough, many American business consultants are calling for more speed in the workplace.

There are many other examples of the value we place on time. Restaurant menu prices may be set not on the cost of the food or of its preparation, but on customers' "renting" table space for all or part of their meal time. Auto repair shops often charge for labor according to a book that lists the average time a given repair is supposed to take.

Time also influences our attitudes toward our jobs:

- Length of the work day: Many employers are offering alternatives to the traditional eight-hour shift, such as flex time, four-day week, and job sharing.
- Shift (day, evening, or night): Workdays begin at different times. Some people like to start work early, because that means they get finished earlier. Others like to work at night.
- Overtime: Many workers count on overtime hours (at a higher rate of pay) to boost their earnings. Others prefer to spend time with friends and family rather than working, regardless of the money.
- Being "on call": Cellular telephones, beepers, and wireless paging systems have made it easier for employers to reach workers. For some people, these devices represent freedom because they don't have to stay in one place or keep calling in when they are away from work. Others see such devices as an unwelcome intrusion into their private lives.
- Sick leave, vacation time, personal leave: To many people, vacation policy or how an employer handles parental leave may be a key factor in their evaluation of the workplace.
- Seniority: Competition for jobs increases as you move up the organizational ladder. When there are fewer opportunities at the top, seniority—how long you have lasted—becomes increasingly important.
- Periodic layoffs: In some businesses, layoffs are a way of life; it's understood that employment is seasonal and workers plan accordingly. They know that they will be recalled eventually and use their "down time" to work on other projects. Long-term layoffs, though, have resulted in enormous economic hardship for families and communities.

➤ Factors related to the job itself: How much rush and waiting the job entails, last-minute deadlines, whether you are given adequate time to do a decent job, whether speed or accuracy is more highly valued all affect our attitudes toward work.

Cycles and Rhythms

We live in a world of cycles, rhythms, and patterns, some of which we barely perceive. A year is a simple and obvious example of a cycle. But other cycles are less obvious.

For example, our level of alertness increases and decreases over a yearly cycle. We are sharpest in the spring and slowest in the summer. Another, less dramatic, peak of alertness occurs in the autumn, followed by a second low point in winter. Many animals follow the same pattern.

People who pay attention to their moods, alertness, creativity, sex drive, and so forth can discover their personal patterns and cycles. Women follow an obvious hormonal cycle of approximately 28 days, but men have cycles, too, though the cycles are not as clearly defined. For example, most men have a daily testosterone cycle, in which testosterone levels rise toward dawn (which explains why so many men wake up with an erection).

A few years ago, a number of books and articles appeared on the topic of biorhythms. This theory suggested that people follow three identifiable cycles: a physical cycle of 23 days, an emotional cycle of 28 days, and an intellectual cycle of 33 days. The theory held that these cycles started at birth. A person who had low points in two or three cycles on the same day was supposedly at risk for accidents or illnesses. However, the biorhythm fad soon faded. There is no scientific evidence that these cycles are valid.

The human body follows circadian rhythms that appear to be regulated by an internal biological clock. Without external cues, such as daylight, alarm clocks, or daily routines, this internal clock tends to run on a 25-hour day.

Circadian rhythms are important because they determine how well a person will adapt to working a late shift or crossing several time zones. Most of us also have 90-minute active–passive cycles during the course of a day. Body temperature, which peaks in the late afternoon and bottoms out in the early morning, is probably the most significant of the circadian rhythms. Along with your metabolic rate, body temperature is responsible for determining whether you are a "lark" or an "owl." Larks are early risers who "hit the ground running," whereas "owls" become alert much more slowly. You can't change your basic biology. The best you can hope to do is adapt, temporarily, to an uncomfortable time schedule.

Another circadian rhythm regulates sleep. Most adults need eight hours of sleep per day. Infants and children need more sleep and older people need less sleep. While we sleep, our bodies move through clearly defined cycles. We have 90-minute dreams and go through several stages of lighter and deeper sleep. One form of migraine headache occurs when the circadian rhythms are altered; some people develop severe "weekend migraines" after staying up very late or sleeping past their usual wake-up time.

Chronobiology is the study of how time affects various organisms, including humans. Scientific researchers in this field are constantly uncovering new explanations for human behavior. They have established a direct link between depression and winter's short daylight hours (seasonal affective disorder, or SAD). They have found evidence that some circadian rhythms make heart attacks more likely to occur in the early morning hours. And they have studied the effects of giving patients medication at different times of the day.

Despite our knowledge of circadian rhythms and patterns of human activity, people continue to feel guilty about the way they utilize time:

- You may feel guilty for sleeping too long or too late.
- If you admit to feeling sleepy early in the evening, you may be teased for being a "party pooper," even though scientific evidence indicates that after age 35 a biological trigger causes many people to become sleepy earlier in the evening.[1]
- You may be criticized for expressing sadness and depression in the middle of the December holiday season.
- Others may find fault with you for not having a lot of energy or being enthusiastic in mid-summer.
- If you question the effects of lack of sleep or early rising, you may be accused of being "too soft."

Many people resist their individual biological patterns:

- Americans constantly complain about lack of sleep, yet many are embarrassed to admit that they'd like to go to bed earlier or sleep longer. In fact, new studies show that more Americans are rising earlier, while their average bedtime has not changed.
- The increase in the number of working women has meant that more children spend their weekdays in child care. As a result, children are awakened earlier in the day. No one knows what the long-term effects of this may be, but teachers and child-care providers may find themselves dealing with more tired and cranky children.
- Instead of trying to accommodate people with different biological rhythms, our jobs often require owls to come to work early and larks to stay up late.

Workshop 5

- Our circadian rhythms allow for alternating periods of activity and passivity during the day, yet many of us have sedentary jobs that require us to remain seated in one place and offer no outlets for releasing pent-up energy.
- Decades of bad jokes and disparaging, sexist remarks have made many women wary about comments on their cycles. For some the subject is so sensitive that it is difficult for them to be objective about how normal hormonal changes affect them.
- People buy, read, and apparently believe in books and articles on time management that offer inappropriate advice such as "add time to your day by getting up 30 minutes earlier."

Other Cycles

Longer cycles may affect our lives. Although they may not directly influence everyone, they can certainly stimulate our curiosity.

- Weather: 22.4 years
- Sunspots: 22.3 years
- Ozone levels: 9 2/3 years
- Animal activity: 9 2/3 years
- Dow Jones average: 41 months
- Real estate prices: 18 1/3 years
- Consumer prices: 54 years
- Drought: 510 years
- Birthdays: 1 year, every year (another measure of aging)

It is interesting to think about the possible connections between human activity and the rhythms of nature. Knowing where we've been might help us predict where we're going.

Not all cycles are related to physics, chemistry, or biology. Others are human constructions set up to organize and structure economic, religious, and social life. Some examples include

- Fiscal year: Calendars for financial planning and budgeting
- School year: Semesters, quarters, trimesters, etc.
- Religious calendars: Often based on solar or lunar cycles, they determine when we celebrate many of our holidays
- Whether you look forward to weekends or can't wait to get back to work on Monday, one of our most important cycles is the seven-day week.

Time and Distance

For thousands of years, humans traveled on foot or on horseback. One way of comparing distances before standards of measurement were developed was to determine how long it took to get there. Before miles and kilometers existed, a "day's journey" was used to measure distance. Although we still use time to measure distance, in the age of automobiles and air travel, a day's journey has shrunk to minutes and a month's journey to hours.

How We Spend Our Time

John Robinson, a sociologist, has studied how people actually spend their time. The ongoing "Americans' Use-of-Time Project" compares the results of studies done in 1965, 1975, and 1985.[2] On the basis of the project's data, it's possible to compare how different populations spend their time. Robinson concluded that large disparities exist in the amount of time men and women spend in housework and child-care activities. Over the course of the 20-year study, some of these figures have changed dramatically (for example, the amount of time women spend working outside the home).[3]

Deadlines

Many people must meet deadlines in the workplace. Although some deadlines are quite reasonable, those that are unreasonable cause problems. If you draw personal satisfaction from your work, you may become upset when you aren't given enough time to do a good job. How should you handle such situations? Ask the person who set the deadline whether the deadline is flexible. When a deadline is firm, there isn't much you can do about it. No matter how unreasonable you think it is, all you can do is grit your teeth and hope that you'll be given more advance notice the next time around. In some businesses, deadlines are considered a major policy decision; at other workplaces, attitudes toward deadlines may be more relaxed. Before you ask for more time to perform a task, find out management's attitudes toward performing work quickly. If your employer gets the impression that you can't keep up with the work load, you may have problems later on.

Planning

Planning is widely touted as a key to success, although excessive planning can detract from spontaneity and limit creativity. The ability to plan is a sign of maturity and mental health. It gives you a measure of power and control over your life as well as an element of stability. Good planners always leave themselves extra time to deal with the unforeseeable. According to Murphy's Law, anything that can go wrong, will go wrong. Therefore allow yourself extra time.

Businesses constantly face the dilemma of how to schedule enough time to complete a job without alienating customers who want something done as soon as possible. Competition is such that businesses need to produce quickly in order to maintain their customer base.

One tool used by business in scheduling is computer technology, which has refined the art of estimating and scheduling. (Some employers have misused computerized estimates to criticize the work done by their employees. This situation may improve as computers become more sophisticated and able to apply "fuzzy logic" to their calculations.)

"Down time" is a major problem in industry. Down time occurs when machinery malfunctions, leaving people and equipment standing idle. One solution is to plan for down time by training workers not just to perform the job (push the button), but to solve problems and to fix and maintain equipment. Companies that are sincerely committed to quality management are able to decrease down time and consequently the cost of having to redo jobs. Workers need to be rewarded not only for speed and accuracy, but for safety and maintenance. If this sounds like common sense, it is.

Schedules and Calendars

There are many different kinds of personal schedules. You may wish to collect samples of daily calendars to show the various formats available. Distribute the "Tips on Schedules and Calendars" handout. Ask participants to discuss the following question: Why is it important to keep a personal calendar?

As promised, we won't spend a lot of time talking about how to make a schedule for yourself. Obviously, the most important reason for recording appointments and events is to keep from forgetting them. A yearly appointment book can also be a powerful planning tool—it can keep you on task and help you avoid distractions. If you have recorded your own plans and commitments, it becomes more difficult for other people to infringe on your time. In addition, you may also feel more psychologically secure just having things written down.

To take control of your time, you may have to become more assertive. You need to decide the extent to which you are willing to protect your time. The following lists some steps you can take:
- Do not permit anyone to alter your schedule without your permission.
- Insist that people make an appointment or let people know that you have set aside specific time each day or week for them to meet with you.
- Refuse to attend meetings if you are not given sufficient advance notice. Don't let people presume that you are free.
- Rethink the need for and timing of regular meetings (replace weekly meetings with biweekly ones, set strict time limits on meetings).

Workplace Stress

- Schedule future meetings before you adjourn.
- Don't let other people's reluctance to plan ahead keep you from making your own plans. Give a deadline to people who say "I can't schedule that far in advance" and explain that if they don't respond you will assume that they do not wish to be included in the plans.

Try to build extra time into your schedule. Save a certain amount of time for yourself. Be aware of your own cycles—your need to periodically recharge your emotional and physical batteries. Some experts say you should reserve 25% of your time for dealing with the unexpected.

Finally, schedule some time for thinking. Too many of us have been led to believe that work gets done by being busy all the time. Thinking and reflecting is a type of work, too.

Games Relating to Time

Chronic Overscheduling

Ask participants to follow along on the "Games People Play with Your Time" handout.

Some people have such a full schedule that they are always running late. Periodically, we all schedule our lives a bit tight, but a person who constantly overschedules his or her time may be playing a psychological game. People who are always rushing from one appointment to the next may be trying to say, "Look how important I am!" and by implication ask others to make allowances for them.

If you have ever had to rely on such a person, you know how frustrating it can be waiting for his or her breathless arrival so that you can get down to business. The only way to deal with someone who insists on playing this kind of game is to *stop playing*.

- Start meetings on time. Let chronic latecomers scramble to catch up on what they have missed. Don't worry about their embarrassment and ignore their excuses.
- Before starting a project, make sure that task priorities are clearly stated so that everyone knows what's important and what isn't.
- Insist on fairness and consistency—refuse to do "special favors."
- Set a firm policy on how many last-minute changes are permitted and specify exactly *when* the last minute is.

Chronic Lateness and Procrastination

People who play chronic lateness and procrastination games use time as a way to control and get back at others. In such games, you are kept waiting helplessly for someone to act, thus making you scramble to make up for lost time. Out of sheer frustration, you may decide to do the job yourself. When you confront someone who is chronically late or a procrastinator, you will find they always have an airtight excuse for why things didn't happen on time and why it is never their fault.

Again, the best way to deal with someone who plays these games is to stop playing the game.

- Don't accept excuses; insist on accountability.
- Make your expectations completely clear from the beginning. If it is necessary to do so, put them in writing and ask others to sign a copy.
- Stop taking on other people's responsibilities. This serves to drive home the important point that they can't rely on you to cover up or make excuses any more.

Conclusion

We started this workshop by looking at different ways to think about time, the value we place on time, and how rhythms and cycles affect us. Then we talked about how to use planning and scheduling to become more protective of our time and energy. We concluded with a discussion of how people play psychological games with time.

Turn to the "Bibliography" handout. An asterisk identifies recommended reading materials. Ask participants to recommend other good books and articles on managing time that are not included in the handout. Urge participants to avoid time-management techniques that make them feel guilty or leave them feeling stupid or inadequate.

Lots of good calendars and schedules are available at bookstores. If you can't find one that meets your particular needs, design your own or hire a graphic artist to custom design one for you. Today people are finding that personal computers are also a great help when it comes to keeping track of dates and appointments.

Don't feel guilty about hiring people to do jobs that you don't have time to do yourself. If a strong sense of obligation causes you to take on too much, think carefully before you say yes. You may even want to get the help of a professional counselor to find out why you can't turn people down. Be creative in finding solutions for your time problems. Enjoy life—you don't have time not to!

References

1. For a fascinating look at cycles and rhythms in our lives, see J. T. Fraser, *Time: The Familiar Stranger* (Amherst, MA: University of Massachusetts Press, 1987).

2. More information about the "Americans' Use-of-Time Project" can be found in John Robinson's regular column, "About Time," in *American Demographics* magazine.
3. John Robinson, "Housework," *American Demographics* 10 (December 1988), p. 24; John Robinson, "Sleeping and Eating," *American Demographics* 11 (November 1989), p. 10; John Robinson, "Childcare," *American Demographics* 11 (July 1989), p. 52.

Handout

Outline for Workshop 5

I. Introduction
II. Time Management—A Popular Topic
    A. Time-management products
    B. Workshop goals
III. Concepts of Time
    A. Age
    B. Where you live
    C. Unwritten rules
    D. Cultural or geographical background
    E. Parents
    F. Psychological state
IV. Value of Time
    A. Time equals money
    B. How time influences our attitudes toward our jobs
V. Cycles and Rhythms
    A. Seasonal cycles
    B. Hormones
    C. Circadian rhythms
    D. Chronobiology
    E. Long-term cycles
VI. Time and Distance
VII. How We Spend Our Time
VIII. Deadlines
IX. Planning
    A. Planning as a sign of maturity and mental health
    B. Planning in business and industry
X. Schedules and Calendars
    A. Becoming assertive to take control of your time
    B. Building extra time into your schedule
XI. Games Relating to Time
    A. Chronic overscheduling
    B. Chronic lateness and procrastination
XII. Conclusion

Workplace Stress

Handout

Tips on Schedules and Calendars

Bookstores and office supply companies offer a large selection of datebooks and personal schedules. If you have a personal computer, various software packages are available for tracking your time. Some inexpensive or free examples include:

- Printers and photocopy shops that create "Things to Do" pads as samples of their work.
- Libraries and bookstores with business forms that can be photocopied or purchased.
- Office, medical, and school supply companies that sell or give away daily reminder booklets or pads.
- Large organizations, corporations, and universities that publish their own calendars to help people coordinate their activities.
- Card and floral shops that give customers pocket calendars.

The calendar you choose is a matter of personal need and taste. If you can't find one that meets your needs, try making your own.

- Use graph paper to lay out your grid just the way you want it.
- Ask someone to proofread it for you (a little protection against Murphy's Law).
- Photocopy your calendar and have it spiral bound with a cover that's tough enough to last.

Other things to consider before picking a calendar:

- A calendar for business should be 18–24 months long.
- The smaller the time increments, the larger the page. In other words, if you schedule appointments every 15 minutes, you'll need a big page. If you work on extended projects, you may use a smaller format showing just A.M. and P.M. for each day.
- Although Sunday is technically the start of the week, some people prefer a calendar that displays the weekend at the end of the week.
- A personal schedule book should include calendars for both the past year and next year and should include all major public and religious holidays.

If the hours printed in your schedule book don't fit with the way you live your life, ignore them. Not every event in life has to start on the hour or half-hour. One supervisor who wanted people to remember meetings scheduled them to begin at odd times, like 9:13. If you wish, write in your own times.

Use a large wall calendar at home for your family to track family and individual activities. Encourage family members to transfer information from their own personal calendars to the large one.

Workplace Stress

Handout

Games People Play with Your Time

Chronic Overscheduling

Some people seem to have such a full schedule that they are always running late. Although we all cut our schedules a bit tight periodically, people who constantly overschedule themselves may be playing a psychological game. People who are always rushing from one appointment to the next are figuratively saying, "Look how important I am!" and by implication asking others to make allowances for them.

If you have to rely on such a person, you know how frustrating it can be waiting for his or her breathless arrival so that you can get down to business. The only sure way to deal with someone who insists on playing this kind of game is for you to *stop playing:*

➤ Start meetings on time. Let chronic latecomers scramble to catch up on what they miss and don't worry about their embarrassment.
➤ Before starting a project, priorities need to be clearly stated and adhered to.
➤ Insist on fairness and consistency—refuse to do special favors.
➤ Set a firm policy on how many last-minute changes are permitted and specify exactly when the last minute is.

Chronic Lateness and Procrastination

Your time is precious and people who play chronic lateness and procrastination games use time as a weapon. In such games you are kept waiting helplessly for someone to act. People who play these games scramble to make up for lost time. Out of sheer frustration, you may decide to do the job yourself. When you confront someone who is chronically late or a procrastinator, he or she always has an airtight excuse as to why things didn't happen on time and it is never that person's fault. Again, the best way to deal with someone who plays these games is for you to stop playing.

➤ Don't accept excuses; insist on accountability.
➤ Make your expectations completely clear from the beginning. If it is necessary to do so, put them in writing and ask the other person to sign a copy.
➤ Stop taking on other people's responsibilities. Make it clear that they can't rely on you to cover up or make excuses any more.

Handout

Bibliography

Time Management

Bliss, Edwin C. (1983). *Doing It Now.* New York: Charles Scribners Sons.
Davidson, Jim (1978). *Effective Time Management.* New York: Human Sciences Press.
Engstrom, Ted W., & R. Alec Mackensie (1967). *Managing Your Time: Practical Guidelines on the Effective Use of Time.* Grand Rapids, MI: Zondervan.
*Gmelch, Walter (1982). *Beyond Stress to Effective Management.* New York: John Wiley.
Hunt, Diana, & Pam Hait (1990). *The Tao of Time: A Revolutionary Philosophy and Guide for Personal Time Management.* New York: Henry Holt.
Kelly, Marjorie (1994, January–February). "You Can't Always Get Done What You Want." *Utne Reader, 61,* pp. 62–66.
Lebov, Myrna (1980). *Practical Tools and Techniques for Managing Time.* New York: Executive Enterprises Publishing.
Mackensie, R. Alec (1990). *The Time Trap.* New York: AMACOM.
Mayer, Jeffrey J. (1990). *If You Haven't Got the Time to Do It Right, When Will You Find the Time to Do It Over?* New York: Simon & Schuster.
Moskowitz, Robert (1981). *How to Organize Your Work and Your Life.* New York: Doubleday.
*Oncken, William (1986). *Managing Management Time: Who's Got the Monkey?* Englewood Cliffs, NJ: Prentice-Hall.
*Simon, Sid (1974). *Meeting Yourself Halfway.* Niles, IL: Argus Communications.
Webber, Ross A. (1972). *Time and Management.* New York: Van Nostrand Reinhold.

Assertiveness and Protecting Your Time

Alberti, Robert, & Michael Emmons (1982). *Your Perfect Right: A Guide to Assertive Living* (4th ed.). San Luis Obispo, CA: Impact Publishers.
*Smith, Donald G. (1976). *How to Cure Yourself of Positive Thinking.* Miami, FL: E. A. Seemann Publishing.
*Smith, Manuel J. (1975). *When I Say "No," I Feel Guilty.* New York: Dial Press.

Thinking about Time, Rhythms, and Cycles

*Fraser, J. T. (1987). *Time: The Familiar Stranger.* Amherst, MA: University of Massachusetts Press.
Rechtschaffen, Stephan (1993, November–December). "Time-Shifting: Slowing Down to Live Longer." *Psychology Today, 25* (6), pp. 32–36.
Updegraff, Robert R. (1958). *All the Time You Need.* Englewood Cliffs, NJ: Prentice-Hall.

Willis, Judith Levine (1990, July–August) "Keeping Time to Circadian Rhythms." *FDA Consumer, 24,* pp. 19–21.

Do-It-Yourself Calendars and Schedules

Lasser, J. K. (1988). *J. K. Lasser's Executives Personal Organizer Forms. J. K. Lasser Tax Institute.* Englewood Cliffs, NJ: Prentice-Hall.

Different Styles of Handling Time

Campbell, Susan (1982). *Beyond the Power Struggle.* San Luis Obispo, CA: Impact Publishers.

*Recommended reading

Handout

Evaluation Form

This workshop covered various ways we think about time and explored two problem areas: errors people make in estimating how much time is needed to do something and games people play relating to time.

Learning Objectives:
- To demonstrate different ways of thinking about time, the value we place on time, and how rhythms and cycles affect us.
- To learn how to use planning and scheduling to become more protective of one's time and energy.
- To understand how people play psychological games with time.

Please respond to these questions by circling the answers you agree with. Your comments will be used to help improve future programs.

1. The presenter fulfilled my expectations of what I wanted to learn from this workshop.

   Very much   Pretty much   Somewhat   Not at all

   Comments:_____
   _____
   _____
   _____

2. I can use the information I obtained in this workshop in my job and/or personal life.

   Very much   Pretty much   Somewhat   Not at all

   Comments:_____
   _____
   _____
   _____

Workplace Stress

3. The presenter knew the material, was organized, and presented the information clearly.

   Very much   Pretty much   Somewhat   Not at all

   Comments:_____
   _____
   _____
   _____

4. What do you wish the presenter had done differently?
   _____
   _____
   _____
   _____

5. What did you like most about this workshop?
   _____
   _____
   _____
   _____

Workshop 6

➤ Protecting Your Time

Learning Objectives

- ➤ To understand different styles of handling time and how these differences can lead to interpersonal conflicts.
- ➤ To show why being overresponsible can cause time-management problems.
- ➤ To review the skills, including assertiveness, needed in order to become more protective of one's time and energy.

Introduction

This workshop is the second of two mini-workshops on time and time management. As in Workshop 5, the material is aimed at giving participants more control over their time and energy. Many recent articles and books on time management talk down to readers and leave them feeling guilty and inadequate. It's insulting to assume that your audience is disorganized, lazy, and full of procrastinators.

This workshop covers how and why people have different styles of handling time, how those different styles can result in interpersonal conflicts, and using assertiveness to become more protective of one's time.

As in the previous workshop, avoid telling workshop participants what they already know. Too many books and articles on time management offer people the same tired old advice: Make a list of what you need to do, determine priorities, do what needs doing. As noted in the introduction to "Making the Most of Your Time" (Workshop 5), this approach is patronizing, serving merely to make people feel guilty and inadequate. It doesn't invite critical analysis of what people put on their lists and why.

Workplace Stress

The workshop begins by looking at how and why people have different styles of handling time. What can be done to reconcile conflicting styles is discussed. The workshop concludes with a discussion of how to protect one's time *assertively*. Distribute handouts and invite participants to follow along using the "Workshop Outline" handout. Tell participants to feel free to ask questions at any time and remind them to turn in their evaluation forms at the conclusion of the workshop.

Handouts

- Workshop Outline
- Time Bibliography (see Workshop 5)
- Assertiveness
- Workshop Evaluation Form

Styles of Managing Time

How you perceive and manage time are influenced in part by your family. However, a growing body of evidence suggests that biology is also a very important influence on how you perceive and manage time.[1] Human behavior is greatly influenced by the internal biological rhythms of the body. Some typical patterns for handling time are more closely related to your "internal clock" than to what you learned in your family.

Life-style

- Jets: These people are often labeled "Type-A" personalities. They are high-energy people who are always in a rush. They usually run on a tight schedule. Jets are often characterized as being ambitious, competitive, and aggressive.
- Horse and Buggy: These folks are more like Type-B personalities and stand in direct contrast with the Jets. Their approach to life is more relaxed and casual. Horse-and-buggy types are more laid back, less directed, and noncompetitive.

Response to Deadlines[2]

- Dawdlers: These people wait until the latest possible moment to do things. They get their tax returns in the mail at midnight on April 15. Sometimes they finish things on time and sometimes they don't. Their work often looks rushed.
- Scurriers: These people do things right away. They believe in getting to the airport hours before their plane leaves, even if it means several hours of boredom.

Daily Rhythms

➤ Larks: These early risers hit the ground running.
➤ Owls: These people become alert more slowly and may not reach their peak of alertness until the afternoon. Larks and owls can't change their basic biological patterns.[3] If you are an owl who must get up early or a lark who must work late, the best you can hope to do is adapt, temporarily, to an uncomfortable time schedule.

Monthly and Annual Rhythms

As the moon revolves around the earth every 28 1/4 days, the ocean tides and weather on earth change. Although women's menstrual cycles are remarkably similar to the moon's cycle, we have no evidence that a connection exists between these two phenomena. Also, many people believe that the phases of the moon, especially the full moon, have a direct effect on human behavior. Again, scientific evidence does not support this belief.

Biological organisms also follow annual rhythms. Animals that sleep through the winter are said to hibernate, whereas those that sleep through the summer estivate. A delicate biological mechanism in the hypothalamus makes us responsive to light and thus to the change of seasons as well. Humans are sensitive to the shorter periods of daylight in winter and stimulated by the arrival of longer days in spring. Other stimuli can also set off psychological triggers that make us aware of the passage of time—for example, the smell of burning leaves in the fall or new-mown grass in the spring.

Opposites Attract

Workshop participants sometimes find characterizations of Jets, Horse and Buggy, Dawdlers, and Scurriers interesting (and amusing) because they reflect relationships in their personal lives. But the potential for serious conflict among such people is obvious, raising the question as to why people with opposite time-management styles form intimate love relationships with each other.

It may sound strange, but many people use their love relationships as tools for managing their time. To understand the dynamics of these relationships, let's look at some of the psychological factors involved.

Sometimes people are attracted to partners whom they sense can help them resolve an internal conflict. For example, a man who is always running late doesn't like being late, but doesn't feel that he can change the way he handles time. When he meets a woman who is always on time (or even a little early), he finds her very attractive. He may sense, subconsciously, that she will be "good for him."

Workplace Stress

If these persons fall in love and wish to develop a good relationship, how can they reconcile their different styles of handling time?
- They can sit down (together or individually) and try to analyze their behavior: Why is he always late? Why does she always need to be punctual? They may find that their conflicting time-management styles are symptoms of more serious problems in their relationship. They may need to become more sensitive to each other's values. Or they may decide that this is not an issue worth fighting about and choose to ignore each other's style.
- They may never resolve their differences. They may fight and argue over who did what, but never find a solution. Sometimes he'll make her late, and sometimes she'll force him to be on time.
- They may try to change each other.
- They may reach a compromise to head off future conflicts. Perhaps they'll decide that each will be individually responsible for getting where he or she needs to be in a timely fashion. Or they may decide that they'll follow his time-management style when going to "his" events and hers when going to "her" events.

If time permits, encourage discussion among workshop participants by asking whether they think a relationship between such polar opposites can succeed. You might also stimulate debate by asking the following questions.

- Is it fair to ask a partner to help you resolve your internal problems with time management?
- How important is it for partners to respect each others' feelings with regard to time-management issues?
- What happens to relationships in which partners can't discuss conflicts such as the one described above?

The Work Ethic and Overresponsibility

It may be very difficult for you to change your perceptions of time when you've been told how to manage your time since childhood. For example,
- You should get up early.
- You should do your laundry on Mondays.
- Working long hours makes you a better person.

Such messages about how you should manage time have become part of the American work ethic. If you have internalized messages such as these, you may feel guilty when you take off work when you are sick or if you sleep late into the morning (even on a weekend or holiday). In small towns or traditional communities, people may feel pressured to do certain things at particular times (for example, don't put up your holiday decorations too soon or don't do your laundry on the "wrong" day). Living by such rigid rules can make you miserable. To break out of this pattern, learn to put things in perspective—to see that these "shoulds" and the values they represent are, for the most part, subjectively determined and aren't chiseled in stone.

If you analyze matters, you may discover that the real problem is your distorted sense of responsibility. Overresponsible people have time-management problems because they're always taking on new obligations.

Because the notion of responsibility varies from person to person, it's difficult to determine whether a particular person has a problem with being overresponsible. What one person might consider a reasonable work load, another might find overwhelming. Generally speaking, though, you're overresponsible when your sense of obligation causes problems for you. When you can't keep up with all the appointments you've made, do all the things you've agreed to do, or find yourself ignoring your own needs because you are so busy taking care of others, you have a problem with overresponsibility.

Why are some people overresponsible? The answer may go back to your childhood. Some children are taught to value overresponsibility (as modeled by their parents), whereas others may use overresponsibility to gain more control over their lives. Some people use overresponsibility to gain power. Some children become overresponsible in an effort to compensate for adults who are irresponsible. Dysfunctional families often play psychological games to get their needs met. Children in such families learn that adults can't be trusted to do what needs to be done. They feel that they must become self-reliant, perform adult tasks, and please adults by meeting adult standards.

If participants have extensive questions about dysfunctional families, the instructor may wish to expand this portion of the workshop. More information about dysfunctional families and overresponsible adults is available from your bookstore or library.

It's not hard to spot the overresponsible people in any group. They're the ones who never say "no" when asked to take on a task. To paraphrase an old saying, "If you want something done right away, ask a busy person to do it."

Waiting and Rushing

Having to wait drives some people crazy and makes them anxious. People don't like having their time controlled by someone else. For example, many people get angry when they're caught in traffic. When we consider that much of our driving time is spent waiting in rush-hour traffic, perhaps America's love affair with the automobile is more myth than reality today.

In a highly competitive service economy, asking customers to wait is a serious problem. Businesses have become so concerned with how customers feel about having to wait that operations research specialists study how people handle waiting. Richard Larson, a "queuing" expert from the Massachusetts Institute of Technology, describes how engineers use techniques such as placing mirrors next to elevators to distract people who are waiting and using "Disneyland lines" that wind back and forth to hide the length of a line.[4] Thus, operations researchers conclude that people's perceptions of "reasonable" waiting time are subjectively determined and can be manipulated.

Some people keep others waiting in order to establish power and authority over them. People who consistently keep others waiting, deliberately or not, are probably playing a psychological game (see Workshop 5).

Rushing people can be as bad as making them wait. People may resent being pressured and having to meet someone else's deadline. In the workplace, this can lead to conflicts between your needs and the organization's rules. You may find yourself asking, "Do they want it done fast or do they want it done right?" Speed is valued in the workplace. Paradoxically, even though people in your department may like it when you expedite a job (even if you have to ignore some of the rules), if someone in another department tries to cut corners, these same people may become righteous and indignant.

Assertiveness

For many reasons, people don't stand up for themselves when others try to take advantage of them. Sometimes the "victim" in such situations is actually playing a psychological game him- or herself. Usually, however, people don't stand up for themselves because:
- They want to be liked and are afraid of making others uncomfortable or angry.
- They feel obligated to remain silent due to the nature of the relationship.
- Being a victim is a familiar and comfortable role, and they don't value (or like) themselves very much.
- They feel insecure, their self-esteem heavily dependent on other people's goodwill, causing them to worry about offending others, making them uncomfortable, or disappointing them.

If you have trouble managing your time, perhaps you are letting people take advantage of you. The best way to protect your time is to become more *assertive*.

Vigorously defending your rights, standing up for yourself, resisting others' attempts to control or manipulate you are all part of becoming assertively protective of your time. Self-protective behavior is considered a sign of mental health and indicates a positive sense of self-worth. Individuals who are unable or unwilling to defend themselves when attacked are often characterized as victims in need of support and assistance.

A person who engages in forceful, attacking behavior is being *aggressive*. Aggression is hostile and can be very destructive. Assertiveness differs from aggression in that it means being persistent and self-confident without being hostile. Use the following guidelines to protect your time:

➤ Remember, you are the only person to whom you must answer for your acts and words.

> Some people worry so much about what others think about them that they live their lives as though every action must be justified and defended. The fear of offending others can be paralyzing—how can you enjoy life if you are constantly afraid of what others may think? If you always feel a need to excuse or explain your behavior, you need to learn to stop justifying everything you do.

➤ People can't take advantage of your feelings or behavior unless you let them. Remember the old saying: "Take advantage of me once, shame on you. Take advantage of me twice, shame on me."

> When you continually let others manipulate you, you give up control over your life and your time. To stop others from using you, you must learn to recognize how their words and actions affect your feelings and behavior. Do they assume that your values are the same as theirs, that your needs and wants are not as important as some other person's? Being assertive means accepting responsibility for making your own decisions about what's important and how you choose to use your time.

➤ Allow yourself to make choices according to the situation. Don't be so bound by tradition that you are unable to adapt to new situations.

> Change is a normal, healthy part of life, but some people will tell you that you have no right to change your mind, that everything you say is chiseled in stone. People who are obsessed with consistency and who insist on adhering rigidly to "the rules" can be difficult to deal with. Times and tastes change, and we all get smarter. Give yourself permission to change your mind without offering excuses or explanations.

➤ Making mistakes is part of being human. No one is perfect.

Perfectionists may try to influence you with their neurotic concern about getting things "just right." In the work world, perfectionism may be translated into demands for "excellence" and "quality" that distort and debase the original meaning of these terms. Resist the temptation to jump on the bandwagon of business fads and buzzwords. Do the best you can and don't buy into the belief that something is wrong with you if you occasionally make a mistake. Use the following two rules to deal with perfectionists: (1) Don't sweat the small stuff and (2) It's all small stuff.

➤ Have the courage to do the right thing even though others may not approve.

Sometimes the only way to solve a problem is to speak the unspeakable or to do the unforgivable. Although it would be wonderful if we could go through life without offending anyone or making anyone uncomfortable, life isn't like that.

Getting along with others is a valuable skill, especially in the workplace, but you don't always need, nor should you expect, the goodwill of others to solve problems effectively. Being assertive means that you weigh your options very carefully before making a decision and that you value the opinions of other people without being afraid that you will offend them by speaking your own mind.

People who try to manipulate others sometimes appeal to the widely held belief that human beings "should" strive for perfection. They insist that you must care about what they care about and that you should want to better yourself and/or "do the right" thing. You have the right to decide what the "right thing" is and to decide not to care about something.

➤ Stop taking responsibility for solving other people's problems.

You may feel compassion for others, but each of us must learn to deal with life's problems and to cope on his or her own. Solving other people's problems teaches them nothing and earns little gratitude. If you want to be a good friend, let the person with the problem accept responsibility (as well as credit) for solving it. When someone needs help, ask yourself this question: "Who owns this problem?" Your obligation to solve the other person's problems should be limited to those situations in which you caused the problem, in which part of your job description is to solve this type of problem, or in which solving the problem will benefit both of you. In other cases, giving your time and energy should be your option.

➤ You can use logic, intuition, or both when solving problems. You should not feel defensive about solutions derived from these methods.

Logic and reason are wonderful tools for solving problems, but they aren't the only tools and aren't always the best tools. Intuition and emotional responses can also help you find human answers to human problems. Even our law courts, with their heavy emphasis on facts and logic, try to temper justice with compassion and mercy.

People who rely solely on logic and reason to solve problems are using only part of their intelligence. Don't feel that you must defend every decision as logical and don't worry about having mixed feelings about people and things.

If more people would accept "Because I felt like it" as an honest explanation, there would be a lot less lying in the world.

➤ Insist that others express themselves openly; if they want something, it should be up to them to ask for it.

Refuse to accept hints and suggestions, especially when others are trying to manipulate you. There's a difference between *manifest* influence, whereby someone gets you to do what they want by explicitly requesting (or ordering) it, and *implicit* influence, whereby you are psychologically conditioned to anticipate the other person's desires in advance.[5] Implicit influence is often the result of the other person treating you like an inferior and your acceptance of that role. Living up to someone else's unspoken expectations can be nervewracking and very hard on your self-esteem.

Who Owns the Problem?

When someone intrudes on your time, *you* have a problem. Until you find a way to point out the effects of this person's behavior, you will own the problem. How can you get someone to help solve a problem that he or she doesn't "own"?

William Oncken observes that new managers in large organizations become swamped with work when they allow subordinates and other managers to pass their tasks to them.[6] Oncken calls this "passing the monkey" onto someone else's back. He advises people to pay close attention to *who's got the monkey* and to learn to protect oneself from those who try to pass their responsibilities onto others. Such advice is probably good in any setting, not just at work.

In discussing why new managers have problems managing their time, Oncken discusses how managers end up doing work that their subordinates ought to be doing. They say things like:

➤ If you want something done right, do it yourself.
➤ I can't ask my subordinates to do anything I'm not ready, willing, and able to do.

Workplace Stress

> ➤ My subordinates need to see frequent examples of how something looks when it's done right.

Instead of facing the responsibilities that come with their position, new managers may use such rationalizations so that they retreat into the familiar. If you are a manager and do your subordinates' work, you are working two jobs. No wonder you feel so pressed for time!

Whether you are a supervisor or manager at work or a responsible parent at home, part of your job is to help your subordinates or children learn to assume responsibility on their own. This is done in several ways. First, you train people to do what needs to be done the way you want it done. Then you begin to give subordinates assignments while offering them increasing freedom to make their own decisions. The more competent they become, the less individual supervision they need and the less of your time they will take.

How much control should you maintain over their work? The first few times your child bakes cookies, you want to be right there in the kitchen, watching his or her every move. The same idea holds true in the workplace. If you feel that you need to maintain control over a job, *assign* it but maintain close supervision.

How many times have you heard people say, "If you want something done right, do it yourself"? To control your time, you must change that way of thinking to "If you want something done right, *delegate it!*"

Your job is to make sure that others understand what you want and expect from them. Delegating responsibility means trusting someone else to do a job right.

Learn to Say "No"

Learn to say "no" if you don't want to do something. In *How to Cure Yourself of Positive Thinking,* Donald Smith discusses how people are coerced by feelings of guilt and obligation to do things they don't really want to do.

> Know, then, what your obligations are, and what they are not, and don't allow yourself to be used. When someone trots out the hoary old line about your duties and responsibilities, tell him that you will make such decisions in regard to yourself and thereby relieve him of the burden of worrying about two people.[7]

Just make sure that saying no doesn't become such a habit that you say no to something you really want to do! It's OK to say yes, as long as *you* are the one who is making the decision. Assertiveness need not make you feel guilty. To say yes should free you to do the things that you really want to do.[8]

Conflicts over Time-Management Styles

How do we resolve conflicts among people with different styles of managing time? The best way to resolve such conflicts is to avoid them in the first place. Start by accepting that we each value different things and have our own ways of handling time. People move at different speeds. You may not especially like the way someone does things, but you can accept their way of doing things as merely different from yours. In the same vein, you needn't cave in to others when they question your way of doing things.

If you supervise the work of someone who has a different time-management style, think about how you will discuss potential problems beforehand. If your goal is cooperation, avoid blaming or criticizing the other person for having a different style. Decide in advance how firm you want to be with this person.

In discussing use of time and deadlines, make sure that others understand that minimum standards exist. For example, a "rush job" is acceptable only if it doesn't look like a rush job. If you can agree about the minimum standards, you can ignore how others achieve these standards.

Other points to remember when trying to resolve conflicts over time-management style:

➤ Set firm deadlines.
➤ Clearly state the penalties for lateness. Spell things out so that there is no room for misunderstanding. For example,

> The payroll department always has to wait for a particular employee to turn in his expense vouchers, which holds up other employees' expense checks. The employee is told when and where vouchers are to be turned in and a new policy is explained: late expense vouchers will not be processed until the next pay period.

➤ Make it clear that no extensions, exceptions, or excuses are allowed.

Beware of people who play games with time, and don't get trapped covering up incompetence. Dealing with serious, chronic time problems is a job for your supervisor (or psychiatrist) to handle.

Conclusion

For more detailed information on time management, refer to the titles listed in the "Bibliography" handout in Workshop 5. A tendency in workshops such as this one, in which time may be limited, is to give participants the impression that making changes in one's life is easy. Participants need to understand that it takes planning, practice, and perseverance to change ingrained habits.

Earlier, we talked about how being overresponsible and feeling obligated can cause time-management problems. On the other hand, responsibility and obligation also help us feel connected to others. Think very carefully before you make major changes in your life. The goal should be to achieve balance.

In this workshop, we explored why people have different styles of handling time and how differences lead to interpersonal conflicts. We examined the question of whether people with opposite styles are attracted to each other and talked about people whose time-management problems stem from feeling overresponsible. We discussed how people feel about having to wait and rush and how to use assertiveness to protect your time and energy.

As a final note, here is Goethe's formula for managing time:

> One ought, every day at least, to hear a little song, read a good poem, see a fine picture, and, if possible, speak a few reasonable words.

References

1. Mary Morse, "We've Got Rhythm," *Utne Reader* 11 (September–October, 1991), p. 24.
2. For a complete discussion of how polar opposites can survive in a love relationship, see Susan Campbell, *Beyond the Power Struggle* (San Luis Obispo, CA: Impact Publishers, 1981).
3. Edward Dolnick, "Snap Out of It," *Health* 8 (February–March, 1992), p. 84.
4. Richard C. Larson, "Perspectives on Queues: Social Justice and the Psychology of Queuing," *Operations Research* 35 (6, 1987), p. 895.
5. Robert Dahl, *Modern Political Analysis* (3rd ed.) (Englewood Cliffs, NJ: Prentice-Hall, 1976), pp. 44–48.
6. William Oncken, Jr., *Managing Management Time: Who's Got the Monkey?* (Englewood Cliffs, NJ: Prentice-Hall, 1986).
7. Donald G. Smith, *How to Cure Yourself of Positive Thinking* (Miami, FL: E. A. Seemann Publishing, 1976), p. 91.
8. For more information about assertiveness, see Robert Aberti and Michael Emmons, *Your Perfect Right: A Guide to Assertive Living* (4th ed.) (San Luis Obispo, CA: Impact Publishers, 1982); Donald G. Smith, *How to Cure Yourself of Positive Thinking*; and Manuel Smith, *When I Say No, I Feel Guilty* (New York: Doubleday, 1975).

Handout

Outline for Workshop 6

I. Introduction
II. Styles of Managing Time
   A. Life-style
      1. Jets
      2. Horse and buggy
   B. Response to deadlines
      1. Dawdlers
      2. Scurriers
   C. Daily rhythms
      1. Larks
      2. Owls
   D. Monthly and annual rhythms
III. Opposites Attract
   A. Love relationships as a way to manage time
   B. Time-management conflicts in relationships
IV. The Work Ethic and Overresponsibility
   A. Messages about how time should be managed
   B. Why people are overresponsible
V. Waiting and Rushing
   A. When your time is controlled by others
   B. Power and authority
   C. Rushing people
VI. Assertiveness
   A. Judge your own behavior
   B. Don't let others take advantage of you
   C. Be flexible
   D. Permit yourself to be less than perfect
   E. Have the courage to do the right thing
   F. Don't take responsibility for solving other people's problems
   G. Use logic and intuition to solve problems
   H. Insist that others speak their minds
VII. Who Owns the Problem
   A. Protecting yourself from people who pass their responsibilities onto others

    B. Helping subordinates and children assume responsibility
    C. Delegating responsibility
    D. Learn to Say "No"
 VIII. Conflicts over Time-Management Styles
    A. Avoid conflicts by accepting others' time-management styles
    B. Avoid blaming or criticizing
    C. Establish minimum standards
    D. Beware of people who play games with time
  IX. Conclusion

Handout

Assertiveness

You may have trouble managing your time if you let people take advantage of you. The best way to protect your time is to become more assertive.

Vigorously defending your rights, standing up for yourself, resisting attempts to control or manipulate you are all part of becoming assertively protective of your time. Self-protective behavior is considered a sign of mental health and indicates a positive sense of self-worth. Individuals who are unable or unwilling to defend themselves when attacked are often characterized as "victims" who need support and assistance.

A person who engages in forceful, attacking behavior is being aggressive. Aggression is hostile and can be very destructive. Assertiveness differs from aggression in that one is persistent and self-confident but not hostile.

- Remember you are the only person to whom you must answer for your acts and words.
- People can't take advantage of your feelings or behavior unless you let them. Remember the old saying, "Take advantage of me once, shame on you. Take advantage of me twice, shame on me."
- Allow yourself to make choices according to the situation. Don't be so bound by tradition that you are unable to adapt to new situations.
- Making mistakes is part of being human. No one is perfect.
- Have the courage to do the right thing, even though others may not approve.
- Stop taking responsibility for other people's problems.
- You can use logic, intuition, or both when solving problems; you need not be defensive about solutions derived from either of these methods.
- Insist that others express themselves openly; if they want something, it should be up to them to ask for it.

Workplace Stress

Handout

Evaluation Form

This workshop covers how and why people have different styles of handling time, how those different styles can result in interpersonal conflicts, and using assertiveness to become more protective of your time.

Learning Objectives:
- ▶ To understand why people have different styles of handling time, which can lead to interpersonal conflicts.
- ▶ To show why being overresponsible can cause time-management problems.
- ▶ To review the skills, including assertiveness, needed in order to become more protective of your time and energy.

Please respond to the following questions by circling the answers that you agree with. Your comments will be used to help improve future programs.

1. The presenter fulfilled my expectations of the workshop.

    Very much   Pretty much   Somewhat   Not at all

Comments: _____
_____
_____
_____

2. I can use the information I obtained in this workshop in my job and/or personal relations.

    Very much   Pretty much   Somewhat   Not at all

Comments: _____
_____
_____
_____

Workshop 6

3. The presenter knew the material, was organized, and presented the information clearly.

   Very much Pretty much Somewhat Not at all

   Comments: _____
   _____
   _____

4. What would you have liked the presenter to do differently?
   _____
   _____
   _____

5. What did you like most about this workshop?
   _____
   _____
   _____

Workshop 7

➤ Why People Burn Out

Learning Objectives

- ➤ To understand what job burnout is and how it affects people.
- ➤ To learn how burnout progresses through three stages.
- ➤ To become more sensitive to the causes of job burnout.

Introduction

In this workshop, the first of two dealing with the problem of job burnout, we will define burnout and examine its causes. Job burnout has only recently been recognized as a serious problem in the American workplace. Burnout has attracted wider attention since it was associated with the long-term effects of job stress. This workshop will try to answer two questions: What is burnout and what causes it? The subsequent workshop, "Preventing and Treating Burnout," deals with how people recover from burnout and what can be done to prevent it.

Distribute and ask participants to complete the "How Burned Out Are You?" handout as a warm-up exercise.

Job burnout has only recently been recognized as a serious problem in the American workplace. In 1981, books and articles began to appear describing burnout among dedicated, experienced professionals. In recent years, the phenomenon has attracted wider attention and become more closely associated with the long-term effects of job stress. This workshop focuses on how burnout affects people and what causes it.

Handouts

- ➤ Workshop Outline

Workplace Stress

- ➤ How Burned Out Are You?
- ➤ Checklist of Burnout Symptoms
- ➤ Burnout Bibliography
- ➤ Evaluation Form

What Is Burnout?

Burnout became a popular topic in the late 1970s and early 1980s, when it was discovered that many of the best people in the "helping professions" (psychology, social work, nursing, teaching, etc.) were quitting at the peak of their careers and moving into unrelated fields. After seven or eight years of helping others, these people were saying things like: "I just don't want to do this anymore." "I'm tired of giving and giving and getting nothing in return." "What's the use? These problems don't go away. People don't get better. Nothing I do seems to make any difference."

At first, the rising dropout rate in the helping professions was attributed to a loss of 1960s idealism. As people get older, it was said, they become more practical and more realistic about the world. However, such commonplace reasoning didn't explain why symptoms of burnout were also found in people who were not in the helping professions and who could not be considered idealistic "do-gooders." In fact, people in all kinds of high-stress jobs were suffering from burnout.

Some people suggested that burnout was the result of a generational character flaw—younger people were perceived as not having the "right stuff" to remain persistent when the going got tough. In truth, however, people of all ages appeared to be susceptible to burnout.

Early authors on burnout were frightened by some of the implications of job burnout. In confronting questions regarding work and the modern-day workplace, they realized that many of the solutions to problems were revolutionary and radical. Afraid of being called radical, many writers backed away from the topic. In the mid-1980s, "burnout" was seldom discussed in books and articles on problems in the workplace. Today, however, burnout is a small part of the flood of materials on "job stress."

As we consider the material in this workshop, we may discover that some situations call for radical solutions. Burnout is a serious problem; it's important to consider all the options available and to keep our minds open to new ideas before coming to any conclusions.

Defining Burnout

Burnout is the name given to a complex set of problems; it represents a lot more than just working too hard and too long. The term is often misused to describe overworked and very busy people as well as people who have been at one job for a long time. Definitions of burnout originated in studies of social workers, nurses, teachers, counselors, physicians, and others. Today, it is believed that burnout affects people with a wide range of vocations, not just the helping professions.

Distribute the "Checklist of Burnout Symptoms" handout and ask participants to follow along. They should check any of the boxes that describe each of the three stages of burnout that apply to their situations.

The term burnout will be used to describe individuals who are no longer able to:
➤ Tolerate the emotional demands of a job
➤ Cope with the daily stresses of the workplace
➤ Muster the energy and enthusiasm needed to do a job well

Burnout usually follows a pattern in which victims go through three stages: emotional exhaustion, depersonalization, and feeling inadequate.[1]

Emotional Exhaustion

Job stress, especially in jobs that require intense social interactions with people, is emotionally draining. In the helping professions, job stress comes from becoming overinvolved in other people's lives, but all jobs to some extent can lead to overwhelming demands on one's time and energy. Emotional exhaustion is the first stage of burnout.

In this stage, you start to feel drained, used up, and without energy. Burnout victims will respond to such feelings by withdrawing and becoming more detached. Instead of working extra hours to get the job done, they will be "out the door by four!" Burnout victims may go from an enthusiastic "can do" attitude to performing the absolute minimum and doing their job strictly "by the book."

By doing the absolute minimum, burnout victims attempt to strike out at or get even with what they perceive to be an unresponsive system. In that sense, their behavior is similar to that of people who play anger games when they don't have a legitimate way to express their unresolved anger. Burnout victims have a lot of unresolved anger.

As burnout worsens, the victim handles problems by sticking to formulaic responses—"Take two aspirins and call me in the morning." The victim's attitudes toward co-workers begin to change, tending toward cynicism and a sense of hopelessness. In some places, burnout victims' attitudes reflect the mistrustful and cynical attitudes of the organization. For example, some organizations have complex procedures for authorizing the allocation of resources, requiring employees to negotiate a lot of red tape to get something done. Although such procedures may be designed to ensure honesty, they also reflect an official attitude that employees can't be trusted.

The instructor might initiate discussion by asking participants how the rules in the workplace reflect the organization's attitudes toward employees and customers.

In some workplaces, attitudes toward clients or customers are negative. They are spoken of as:
- Stupid and lazy
- Abusive and demanding
- Crooks and swindlers
- Not to be trusted

Working in such negative environments can be physically and emotionally draining. Over time, the worker lacks the energy to care, which leads to the next stage of burnout—depersonalization.

Depersonalization

In the second stage of burnout, people become indifferent to co-workers and/or customers. The burnout victim may become increasingly cynical, cold, and hostile.

Burnout victims are often aware that something is happening to them. They can see themselves changing but feel helpless to stop it. They feel distressed about the poor job they are doing and guilty for not caring anymore. They feel like a failure and do not like themselves very much.

Feeling Inadequate

Eventually, the burnout victim feels completely inadequate to do the job and feels like a fraud, failure, and "loser."

Loss of self-esteem results. Burnout victims tell themselves "I'm worthless" or "I'm useless." People get a lot more than a paycheck from their work. Such negative self-messages are very debilitating over time.

How is your self-esteem tied to the work you do? Does work fulfill your need to be needed, to be loved, to feel useful, to experience satisfaction? The following are examples of how self-esteem and work are interrelated.
- Graduation: Finishing your formal education leaves you feeling pretty good about yourself.
- Job hunting: Looking for a job can be hard on your self-esteem.
- Finding a job: After you find a job you begin to feel better about yourself.
- Starting a new job: Discovering how much you still have to learn can be bewildering.
- Training: As you learn through on-the-job training, you become more comfortable with and confident in yourself.
- Competence: After completing your training, you feel good about yourself.

If the workplace undermines your sense of hard-earned self-esteem, you begin to lose confidence and may feel depressed due to your inability to affect your work environment. Such feelings are frequently accompanied by anger at yourself for having failed.

Now go back to the opening exercise and review your responses to the handout "How Burned Out Are You?" Can you determine the stages you have gone through and the symptoms you have experienced?

Spotting a Burnout Victim

Subjective signs[2]
- Emotional exhaustion
- Feelings of failure and frustration
- Decline in self-esteem
- Feeling trapped
- Feeling bored

Physical signs
- Increasing fatigue
- Sleep disturbance
- Change in appetite (for food, drink, sex)
- Lowered resistance to infections
- Headaches

Behavioral signs
- Skipping rest and/or food breaks
- Delaying or canceling vacations or trips

Other behaviors and attitudes that identify burnout sufferers include the following:[3]
- Unwarranted feelings that one is indispensable
- An unrealistic sense of omnipotence
- Denial of feelings (especially negative ones) that are obvious to others
- Sometimes acting disoriented

If you have doubts about whether you're burned out, ask your friends and colleagues for their opinions. Listen to what they say!

Solutions That Don't Work

Victims of burnout feel themselves becoming more and more emotionally exhausted with each passing week. The more unhappy they become with their lives, the more desperate they are to find a cure for what ails them. In their desperation, they sometimes resort to poor coping mechanisms:
- To revive their interest and enthusiasm, they may try to work harder, putting in longer hours and taking on more tasks.

Workplace Stress

- They may resort to using alcohol or drugs to reduce their emotional pain.
- Seeking stimulation, they may get caught up in risky and self-destructive behaviors such as extramarital affairs, gambling, or excessive spending.

Burnout victims find it increasingly difficult to unwind after work, and stress moves from work to home. Relationships with spouse, children, family, and friends begin to suffer.

What Causes Burnout?

Many have sought to explain why people burn out. Some of their theories may seem more plausible than others. The following lists some theories as to why people burn out:

Ask participants to share their ideas regarding why people burn out on the job. Ask them to think of people who have burned out and to consider what caused the problem. Explain that their theories may be as valid as those of the experts.

- People may burn out if their expectations of a job are unrealistic, if they expect to accomplish too much, or if they expect a job to be more exciting and interesting than it really is.
- People who have interesting and exciting jobs sometimes have to deal with periods of high stress and periods of drudgery. As long as boredom and excitement are balanced, the job is bearable, even enjoyable. Burnout may occur when that balance is disturbed and the individual finds the combination of stress and boredom overwhelming.
- Burnout may result from carrying too many work-related problems into other areas of one's life. People who are good at leaving their work problems behind at the end of the day are less likely to burn out. They are able to "compartmentalize" their lives: When they are at work they deal only with work; at home, they deal with domestic responsibilities.
- In many jobs, workers don't have the opportunity to work on a project from start to finish. Workers who never get to see the result of their labor or who have to depend on others to complete a project may be more likely to burn out. They don't get the sense of accomplishment that comes from completing the job on their own.
- The problem may be situational—that is, it may lie in the nature of the workplace. This was one of the first (and most widely discussed) theories advanced to explain burnout, so we will examine it more closely.

Nature of the Workplace

For some workers, the problem is situational and lies in the nature of the workplace. Many people wrongly assume that there's something "wrong" with a person who burns out, that he or she is weak or lacks ambition and drive. However, there is a tendency to overestimate the importance of personal factors and to underestimate the importance of the situation or environment.[4]

In other words, don't ask who burns out, ask where people burn out. Analyze the work environment to determine whether it may be contributing to burnout.

- What tasks are you asked to perform?
- Do you have to turn people down a lot? Some jobs require workers to perform unpleasant tasks or ask embarrassing questions.
- What restrictions and rules do you have to follow? Are the organization's plans, policies, and procedures flexible?
- Do policies and procedures keep you from being effective? Do they make your job harder or easier to do?
- Do you have some discretion regarding what tasks you handle?
- Are you overloaded with tasks?
- Are time limits and deadlines reasonable or arbitrary?
- Do deadlines force you to lower your standards?
- Do you receive feedback on your work?
- What are the nonmonetary rewards for success in your work? What do you find most satisfying about your work?
- Is the workplace clean and safe?
- Do you have privacy when you need it?
- Are equipment and machinery kept in good condition?
- Are supplies or equipment difficult to obtain?
- Are your co-workers supportive or critical of you?
- Are employees afraid to rock the boat?
- Does the work "culture" encourage "toughing it out" and "suffering in silence"?
- Are supervisors helpful or a hindrance?

Stress, Burnout, and the Performance Curve

Burnout results from chronic, daily stress, rather than from occasional crises. Although crises can be very stressful, they are usually resolved. Chronic stress, however, is inescapable. The emotional stress of working in a nonsupportive environment grinds away at people's tolerance and their ability to cope.

We all need *some* stress in our lives; without stress life would be unbearably boring. When people do not have enough stimulation in their life, they may suffer from "rust out." If burnout (excessive stress in your life) represents one end of the "performance curve," then rust out (too little stress) represents the other.

Workplace Stress

Most people have an *optimum* level of stress, meaning that they function best when faced with a certain level of difficulty and challenge. When we are receiving the optimum amount of stimulation, we are said to be near the peak of the performance curve; our problem-solving skills are better, we have more creative energy, we can initiate change and make progress toward our goals, and we derive more satisfaction from our work.

What is stress and how does it affect burnout? Stress is defined as your body's nonspecific response to a demand that it cope with change, whether physical, emotional, or both (see Workshop 1). You may respond to the change physically and/or emotionally. For example, when you feel cold, your body experiences stress, causing you to do something—get a jacket, pull out another blanket. If your co-worker takes advantage of you, you may become angry and consequently feel emotional stress. Stress may be caused by pleasant events (having the family over for Thanksgiving dinner) as well as unpleasant events (a death in the family).

Rust Out

If a job has too little stress and stimulation, it becomes dull and boring. Some people don't mind this. "It's just a job," they might say. "This is what I do for a paycheck; my 'real life' starts after I punch out for the day."

But other people are uncomfortable in such work situations and may find "creative" ways to fight the monotony. One skill necessary for surviving in a low-stimulation job is to avoid looking bored. Some of the techniques people use to fight boredom are nonproductive or harmful to morale. Also, bored workers may play psychological "games" to stir up conflicts.

Over time, a bored worker may become restless, frustrated, and resentful. If you find yourself in this position, you may feel that your skills and intelligence are being wasted. Decide whether you are ready to start looking for another job before you rust out or get yourself fired.

Job Stress and Burnout

Researchers have found two key elements that can cause job stress to lead to burnout.

The first factor is *unpredictability*. Jobs in which the person never knows what's going to happen next have the highest levels of burnout. Jobs that are unpredictable and require you to change gears too frequently are exhausting.

The second factor leading to job stress and burnout is the degree of *control* you have over your work. It is extremely important to have an escape valve whereby you can vent pent-up feelings and/or get away from a stressful job situation. You need room to maneuver and flexibility to try different options so that you don't feel trapped and helpless.

Feeling out of control leads to burnout. Being forced to follow procedures, having no input in policy decisions, and feeling that you have no escape from responsibilities all add to feelings of helplessness.

In the helping professions, two other factors are related to burnout and job stress. Empathy is especially valued among helping professionals, but too much empathy can lead to overidentifying with the people whom you are trying to help. This can lead to a loss of objectivity. The helper loses track of who "owns" the client's problems and who has responsibility for solving them. Identifying too closely with the people whom you are trying to help can result in your adding their problems to your own.

If the focus of your work with people is always on problems, you may start to see people in negative terms. Helping professionals who work with highly troubled populations such as criminals, rapists, child molesters or abusers, addicts, and abusive people who take their frustrations out on the helper; the chronically sick or terminally ill; sociopaths; the severely depressed; or suicidal people experience extremely high levels of stress.

It is also very stressful to work in a situation in which little hope for change or improvement exists. In some cases, people will solve a set of problems, yet their lives won't get any better. You may feel that your time and energy are being wasted and thus experience frustration. Dealing with chronic problems and long-term dysfunctions can lead to job burnout.

Conclusion

There is no way to predict with any accuracy who will burn out at a given job. Every year, many highly trained, experienced workers burn out, leave their jobs, and begin new careers. When they take their expertise with them without passing it along to others, we all lose.

The goal of this mini-workshop was to make you aware of the problem in the hope that you may be able to avoid burnout. The "Burnout Bibliography" handout lists a number of resources that you may find helpful. Admitting that you are having trouble maintaining your interest and enthusiasm for a demanding job is not shameful. You have the right to have your feelings respected by supervisors, co-workers, and clients.

References

1. Christina Maslach, *Burnout: The Cost of Caring* (Englewood Cliffs, NJ: Prentice-Hall, 1982), p. 3.

2. For more information on the subjective signs of burnout, see Pamela Patrick, *Health Care Worker Burnout* (Alexandria, VA: Inquiry Books, 1980).
3. For more information on the attitudinal signs of burnout, see Herbert Freudenberger, with Geraldine Richelson, *Burnout: The High Cost of High Achievement* (Garden City, NY: Anchor Press, 1980).
4. Maslach, *Burnout: The Cost of Caring,* p. 10.

Handout

Outline for Workshop 7

    I. Introduction
   II. What is Burnout?
      A. Popular topic in the late 1970s and early 1980s
      B. Loss of 1960s idealism
      C. A generational character flaw
      D. Revolutionary and radical solutions to burnout
  III. Defining Burnout
      A. Emotional Exhaustion
      B. Depersonalization
      C. Feeling inadequate
  IV. Spotting a Burnout Victim
      A. Subjective signs
      B. Physical signs
      C. Behavioral signs
      D. Other attitudes and signs
   V. Solutions That Don't Work
      A. Working harder
      B. Alcohol or drugs
      C. Risky and self-destructive behaviors
  VI. What Causes Burnout?
      A. Unrealistic job expectations
      B. Periods of high stress and drudgery
      C. Carrying work-related problems home
      D. Never seeing the results of your labor
      E. Work environment
 VII. Stress, Burnout, and the Performance Curve
      A. Chronic stress
      B. Optimum level of stress
      C. Rust out
      D. Job stress and burnout
         1. Unpredictability of the work environment
         2. Control over your work
         3. Helping professions and overidentification with others
VIII. Conclusion

Workplace Stress

Handout

How Burned Out Are You?

Rate each item using the following scale: 0 = Doesn't apply, 1 = Never, 2 = Rarely, 3 = Sometimes, 4 = Often, 5 = Always.

1. [ ] It takes longer to unwind at the end of the work day than it used to.
2. [ ] I worry about work at night and have trouble sleeping.
3. [ ] I don't like telling people what I do for a living.
4. [ ] My job responsibilities overwhelm me.
5. [ ] I suffer from headaches, stomachaches, or lower back pain.
6. [ ] I feel I am no longer effective at my job.
7. [ ] I get angry and irritated more easily.
8. [ ] I feel that people don't appreciate me—they "use" me.
9. [ ] Even when I get enough sleep, I still feel exhausted.
10. [ ] I dread going to work.
11. [ ] I'm comfortable using labels when talking about the people I work with.
12. [ ] It's becoming harder to empathize with the people I work with.
13. [ ] I apply the "rules" much more strictly than I used to.
14. [ ] I spend a lot of time at work just watching the clock.
15. [ ] I lump the people I work with into categories, sometimes before I have all the facts.
16. [ ] My use of tobacco, drugs, and/or alcohol has increased lately.
17. [ ] I make "sick" jokes about the people I deal with at work.
18. [ ] I miss more than a day of work per month.
19. [ ] Many of the attitudes I express at work are cynical or negative.
20. [ ] Before I started this job, I had no idea what I was getting myself into.
21. [ ] I am sometimes confused about what I am supposed to be doing for the people with whom I work.
22. [ ] My boss's skills are totally inadequate for his/her position.
23. [ ] I have to make all the decisions around my office.
24. [ ] When I think about trying to change the system, it seems hopeless.
25. [ ] I get my emotional needs met almost entirely by my job and my colleagues.
26. [ ] Too much paperwork keeps me from doing a good job.
27. [ ] Stressed-out people are usually too upset to make important decisions.
28. [ ] I feel responsible for handling everything I'm asked to do at work.
29. [ ] There's a rule for every situation and every situation fits a rule.
30. [ ] I feel that I must respond to every request, no matter who makes it.

31. [ ] My job consists of so many different tasks that I feel overwhelmed.
32. [ ] I spend a lot of time with co-workers after hours.
33. [ ] I have not been adequately trained in dealing with people.
34. [ ] My salary is much lower than it should be.
35. [ ] I'm not involved in any kind of support system of people in my field.
36. [ ] Our budget is never big enough to do what we're supposed to do.
37. [ ] My work load is much too big for one person.
38. [ ] I often work long shifts or put in a lot of overtime.
39. [ ] I have never been given a reliable set of guidelines for my job.
40. [ ] I don't take time for breaks, lunch, illness, or vacations.

Less than 40: You're in pretty good shape and have a minor amount of job stress.

40 to 80: Your level of job stress is manageable and you are not likely to burn out.

81 to 120: You may be able to avoid burning out if you have good stress-management skills and solid self-esteem.

121 to 160: You are under a lot of job stress and may have already begun to burn out.

Greater than 161: You are under enormous job-related stress and in an advanced stage of burnout.

Adapted with permission from Martha Bramhall and Susan Ezell, "How Burned Out Are You?" *Public Welfare* 39 (Winter 1981), p. 26.

Workplace Stress

Handout

Checklist of Burnout Symptoms

Burnout is indicated by a set of symptoms that appear in individuals who are no longer successfully coping with job stress. A person is burned out when he or she is no longer able to:
➤ Tolerate the emotional demands of a job
➤ Cope with the daily stresses of the workplace
➤ Muster the energy and enthusiasm to do a job well.

Burnout victims suffer from emotional exhaustion, depersonalization, and reduced personal accomplishment. Burnout is a response to the chronic emotional strain of dealing with other people, particularly people who are having serious social or psychological problems. Check the items that apply to you.

Emotional Exhaustion
[ ] I'm under a lot of job stress, mostly from having to deal with people.
[ ] I feel drained, used up; I lack energy.
[ ] Instead of trying to solve problems, I do the bare minimum.
[ ] I usually take the easiest way out—use a "formula"—instead of using my skills or intelligence.
[ ] I often feel that I am very close to reaching my limits.

Depersonalization
[ ] I don't view the people I work with as "real people" any more.
[ ] I can't bring myself to care about my co-workers' problems.
[ ] I feel that I've lost my touch at work. This distresses me, but I can't help it.
[ ] I feel guilty because I don't care any more.
[ ] I feel like a failure. Nothing I do really helps.
[ ] I wish I could quit.

Reduced Sense of Personal Accomplishment
[ ] I'm not really doing much—just hanging in there.
[ ] I'm pretty worthless and feel useless.
[ ] I feel angry for failing.
[ ] I feel helpless to fix myself.
[ ] Everything about my job depresses me.

Handout

Burnout Bibliography

Cherniss, C. (1980). *Staff Burnout: Job Stress in the Human Services*. Beverly Hills, CA: Sage Publications.

Freudenberger, Herbert J., with Geraldine Richelson (1980). *Burnout: The High Cost of High Achievement*. Garden City, NY: Anchor Press.

Freudenberger, Herbert J. (1982). "Counseling and Dynamics: Treating the End-Stage Person." In W. S. Paine (Ed.), *Job Stress and Burnout*. Beverly Hills, CA: Sage Publications.

Freudenberger, Herbert J., & Gail North (1985). *Women's Burnout: How to Spot It, How to Reverse It, and How to Prevent It*. Garden City, NY: Doubleday.

Gmelch, Walter H. (1982). *Beyond Stress to Effective Management*. New York: John Wiley.

Jaffe, Dennis, & Cynthia D. Scott (1988). *From Burnout to Balance*. New York: McGraw Hill.

Maslach, Christina (1982). *Burnout: The Cost of Caring*. Englewood Cliffs, NJ: Prentice-Hall.

Maslach, Christina (1982). "Understanding Burnout." In W. S. Paine (Ed.), *Job Stress and Burnout*. Beverly Hills, CA: Sage Publications.

Paine, Whiton Stewart (Ed.) (1982). *Job Stress and Burnout: Research, Theory, and Intervention Perspectives*. Beverly Hills, CA: Sage Publications.

Patrick, Pamela (1980). *Health Care Worker Burnout*. Alexandria, VA: Inquiry Books.

Pines, Ayala, & Eliot Aronson (1981). *Burnout: From Tedium to Personal Growth*. New York: Free Press.

Pines, Ayala, & Eliot Aronson (1988). *Career Burnout: Causes and Cures*. New York: Free Press.

Walker, J. Ingram (1980). *Everybody's Guide to Emotional Well-Being*. New York: Harbor Publishing.

Workplace Stress

Handout

Evaluation Form

Job burnout has only recently been recognized as a problem in the American workplace. It has attracted much wider attention since its association with job stress. This workshop attempts to answer two questions: What is burnout? What causes it?

Learning Objectives:
➤ To understand what job burnout is and how it affects people.
➤ To understand how burnout progresses through three stages.
➤ To become more sensitive to the causes of job burnout.

Please respond to the following questions by circling the answers with which you agree. Your comments will be used to help improve future programs.

1. The presenter fulfilled my expectations of what I wanted to learn from this workshop.

   Very much   Pretty much   Somewhat   Not at all

   Comments: _____
   _____
   _____
   _____

2. I can use the information I obtained in this workshop in my job and/or personal relations.

   Very much   Pretty much   Somewhat   Not at all

   Comments: _____
   _____
   _____
   _____

Workshop 7

3. The presenter knew the material, was organized, and presented the information clearly.

   Very much   Pretty much   Somewhat   Not at all

   Comments: _____
   _____
   _____
   _____

4. What would you have liked the presenter to do differently?
   _____
   _____
   _____
   _____

5. What did you like most about this workshop?
   _____
   _____
   _____
   _____

Workshop 8

➤ Preventing and Treating Burnout

Learning Objectives
- ➤ To explore the various choices of burnout victims who want to counter this condition.
- ➤ To learn how to develop a plan for recovering from burnout.
- ➤ To understand the changes that can be made to prevent future burnout.

Introduction

Over the course of several years, job burnout causes a marked decline in the quality of a person's work. Victims of burnout go from being competent, enthusiastic problem solvers to uninterested, unmotivated pencil pushers who are unable and unwilling to expend more than the minimum amount of time or energy on the job. Many factors, including personality, ability to handle stress, personal expectations, and the work environment, contribute to burnout.

In Workshop 7, we looked at what burnout is and how it affects people. In this workshop, we will talk about burnout prevention and overcoming burnout.

Handouts
- ➤ Workshop Outline
- ➤ How to Keep from Burning Out
- ➤ Managing to Prevent Burnout
- ➤ To Whom It May Concern
- ➤ Burnout Bibliography (see handout for Workshop 7)
- ➤ Evaluation Form

Workplace Stress

Overcoming Burnout

Job burnout is a condition whereby various situations, events, or factors lead to a marked decline in the quality of a formerly competent individual's work. Burnout victims lose their energy and enthusiasm over the course of several years until they are no longer able to maintain the motivation and creativity they had when they began their job.

People who have reached the most advanced stages of job burnout may not be able to recover completely. If you've reached the end stage of burnout—emotionally exhausted, unable to deal with people as individuals, and no longer feeling a sense of personal accomplishment from your work—it's unlikely that anything short of a complete job change will allow you to restore your energy. The only effective solution for total burnout is to get out of your present job environment and find some way to enjoy the rest of your life.

Depending on your level of burnout, the following describes actions you can take to recover. Basic stress-management techniques can help. Learn at least one technique for coping with stress, such as relaxation, meditation, or biofeedback (see Workshop 1 for more ideas on coping with stress). You also need to identify the stressors in your life, then decide which ones you can live with and which ones you'll need to change.

When work begins to wear you down, learn to "work smarter, not harder."[1]

- Set realistic goals for yourself. Try to be specific about these goals; if you don't know when you've reached your goal, how will you know when to stop? Be realistic and don't bite off more than you can chew.
- Try doing things differently. Vary your daily and weekly routines when it is possible to do so to keep your job interesting and to help you develop a sense of control over your work.
- Take breaks. Even short breaks can help you get away from your stressors. When you are on a break, don't work, and don't let other people invade your time with work-related problems. The same holds true for your lunch period, weekends, and vacations. You need these times to recharge your batteries. Protect your time!

If you work in front of a video display terminal (VDT), it's especially important that you take regular breaks away from your work station. Controversy still exists about the possible health dangers of working at a VDT. Some studies suggest that VDTs pose a serious threat to workers' health from radiation, repetitive motion, eyestrain, and back problems. The U.S. government recommends that people who work at a VDT take a minimum of one 15-minute break (away from the screen and keyboard) every two hours. If you're concerned about the safety of working at a VDT, contact the manufacturer or the Occupational Safety and Health Administration (OSHA).

- Learn to leave your work at work. Get away from work-related problems. Develop after-work outlets through hobbies, sports, and other forms of play. Make having fun a priority in your life.
- Don't take things personally and don't overidentify with the workplace. If your customers, clients, or co-workers are angry, understand that they are probably frustrated with the system, not you.

A good support system is very important for someone trying to overcome burnout. Your peers can help in many ways.

- In addition to offering you direct aid, co-workers can be a source of advice, information, and comfort when things get rough.
- They may be able to give you insights into your work that help you keep things in perspective.
- Co-workers may help you compare your feelings with theirs.
- Co-workers may be your main source of positive feedback.
- Humor can help you survive in a stressful job situation. However, beware of humor that uses cruel teasing or ridicule, which may indicate that people are dealing with high levels of anger. Such anger can result in nasty anger games (see Workshop 4).

If you are isolated or work alone, you may have problems finding adequate peer support. Here are some ways to solve this problem:

- Attend conferences and gatherings of people in your field. You'll meet people who are in the same circumstances and may be able to learn how they have managed to avoid burnout.
- Contact others in your situation via telephone, mail, fax, or computer bulletin boards and electronic mail.
- Read trade journals and magazines to learn how others cope and solve problems.
- If resources are not available, you might want to pay a consultant or psychotherapist to give you feedback, help you solve problems, and stay in touch with reality.

Developing a Plan to Overcome Burnout

To recover from burnout you may have to make changes in your life in order to break out of old patterns. The effort required to make changes, if you are in the advanced stages of burnout, may seem impossible. Change may seem so difficult, so impossible to attain, and so exhausting that you don't even want to think about it. Burnout victims resist change, because making changes is difficult and stressful, even if that is the only way to overcome burnout.

Paradoxically, burnout is often associated with high levels of stress, which result from having to cope with physical, psychological, and emotional changes. For a burnout recovery plan to be effective, it must take into account the stress that may result from having to make changes in one's life.

Martha Bramhall and Susan Ezell created a treatment plan to overcome burnout.[2] This model requires you to make some changes, but it also allows you to take things one step at a time instead of trying to do it all at once. The plan suggests that you cut back on your most stressful activities and to stop overworking as compensation for feeling burned out.

Supervisor's Cooperation

What can you expect from your supervisor if you tell him or her that you are suffering from job burnout? Before you begin developing your burnout recovery plan, consider the "official" attitude in your workplace toward burnout. In some circles, burnout carries a stigma—being burned out means that something is wrong with you. Try to determine whether you'll be seen as weak or incompetent if you admit you need help overcoming burnout. Will you be expected to deal with it yourself or will your supervisors and co-workers try to help you recover? To implement your burnout recovery plan, you'll need your supervisors' cooperation.

It's extremely important for persons trying to recover from burnout to enlist the support of their supervisor. The "To Whom It May Concern" handout provides participants with a guide for discussing burnout with a supervisor or co-worker. Similar to the "Burnout Checklist" used in Workshop 7, it allows the individual to demonstrate directly the extent to which he or she feels burned out. Participants may wish to discuss how they think their supervisors would react to the "To Whom It May Concern" letter. Some supervisors will respond sympathetically, whereas others will not. Participants need to weigh the advantages and disadvantages of discussing job burnout with a supervisor.

Cutting Back

Ideally, you should try to cut in half the amount of time you spend working with people and their problems. This may not be feasible, but you can try several strategies.

Ask your supervisor whether your most draining tasks can be shared, temporarily, with your co-workers. If your colleagues resent this, explain your situation to them. Tell them that, at this point, you can't "pull your weight" and that you intend to be back on your feet and doing your fair share of the work as soon as you can.

Put your energy into only the most pressing job responsibilities and situations. Work out an arrangement that allows you to give brief oral reports instead of spending energy doing paperwork. Write short memos to yourself so that you don't lose track of what you've done. These can be incorporated into longer written reports later on, if you wish to do so.

Rest

Use sick time, if you must, to get some rest and relaxation and to resolve problems in your personal life. It is not recommended that you take an extended leave of absence, because that won't result in behavioral changes at work and will probably only delay your descent into burnout.

Take 15-minute breaks as often as you can during the day. Spend your break time alone. Practice relaxing.

Get at least eight hours of sleep at night. If you feel guilty about spending time in bed, remind yourself that getting enough sleep is a health issue and that value judgments of others are irrelevant at this point in your life. If you have problems falling asleep or staying asleep, seek medical help or consult a sleep disorders clinic for help.

Exercise

Exercise a little bit every day. Make exercise relaxing; don't overdo it. As a burnout victim, you need all the energy you can muster.

Developing Outlets for Your Feelings

Find a friend or co-worker in whom you can confide and talk about your feelings, with the understanding that at this point, you may not have the patience or energy to do the same for him or her. Let friends help you work toward understanding your burnout. Take some time to mourn the loss of your idealism and give yourself permission to grieve. If you feel a lot of unexpressed anger, tap into the energy that anger produces to make some positive changes in your life.

Psychotherapy may not be useful for someone in an advanced stage of burnout. Therapy can work better after you're on the road to recovery and have more energy to put into personal-growth issues.

Eating

Burnout victims tend to consume a lot of caffeine and refined sugar to help them keep going. A better choice is to use less caffeine, switch to a diet high in protein, and eat six small meals a day—rather than two or three large meals—to keep your blood sugar level constant. Foods to avoid when under a lot of stress include carbohydrates, refined sugar, salt (sodium), and high-fat junk foods.

Alcohol will not make it easier for you to overcome burnout, and if you use alcohol for an extended period, you may become dependent on it. The same can be said for many nonprescription drugs and medicines people take to relieve the symptoms of stress. The newest generation of antidepressant medicines may help some victims of burnout; ask a physician for recommendations.

Learn to Say "No"

If you don't feel up to doing something, you'll have to learn to say "no." Being overextended and feeling obligated may be part of why you burned out. Recognize your limits and give yourself permission not to do things. Accept "I don't want to" as a perfectly legitimate reason.

Asking for Help

Someone who has been self-reliant and self-confident may find asking for help difficult to do. It isn't easy admitting to your supervisor that you can no longer "cut it." Your supervisor may resist the idea that someone with your skills and experience has lost his or her touch.

If your supervisor won't deal with your problem, you may need to convince him or her that you aren't disposable and that you deserve to be treated like a person who needs some help to recover from a health problem. Point out that the cost of replacing you will be high; training and finding someone to handle your work load could be costly to your employer.

Although your co-workers might resent your special needs, you can explain that if it can happen to you, it can happen to them. Asking for help is part of the healing process. It's a positive sign that you care about yourself; it's good for your self-esteem.

Bailing Out

In some instances "sticking it out" in a bad situation may have adverse effects on co-workers, customers, family members, and your own health and well-being. Being burned out doesn't relieve you of your responsibilities. It's still your responsibility to get the job done. It isn't fair to let others become victims of your burnout.

Sometimes the only intelligent decision may be for you to quit your job. Quitting a job because of burnout is no disgrace; it may be the only logical response to an untenable situation.

You may not have to completely abandon your training and experience. Explore the possibility of moving up to an administrative position or laterally to different job responsibilities. Many people who are studying toward advanced degrees in the helping professions are burnout victims trying to remain in the field without the stress of dealing with the devastating problems of certain kinds of clients.

Preventing Burnout

What can be done to prevent good people from becoming victims of burnout? Some experts think that burnout prevention should start at the very beginning of one's vocational training. From the moment you choose to enter a high-stress occupation, particularly one that will require you to spend a lot of time working with people and their problems, you should be trained to recognize the symptoms of burnout.

Persons at Risk

Identifying who is at risk for burnout is difficult. Many people label burnout victims as weak-willed, quitters, or worse, without knowing anything about burnout. Although it's unfair to label people, it should be noted that several personal factors seem to correlate with greater risk of burnout. Unrealistic expectations of a career or workplace can make a person susceptible to burnout. Excessive idealism and dedication can blind people to the realities of their work situation, causing stress that leads to burnout.

The personal characteristics that once made burnout victims so good at their jobs may eventually make them vulnerable to burnout. For example, burnout victims tend to be high-energy people who are very competent, accomplished, self-sufficient, and independent. Sometimes people who have little self-confidence compensate by being overresponsible. These people are unable to say "no," and their lives are often overscheduled.

Although researchers have found few significant demographic factors that distinguish persons who are likely to burn out from the general population, some experts believe that a burnout-prone personality can be recognized. They claim that burnout is more likely to occur among persons who are unassertive when dealing with people.[3] These people are ideal "team players"—submissive and anxious to please. Their personal goals are unclear, so they acquiesce and adapt to the wishes of others. Their self-esteem comes through winning approval and acceptance from others.[4]

Burnout victims have been characterized as being fearful of involvement, having trouble setting limits on their relationships, being controlled by situations (reacting rather than initiating), and being impatient and intolerant of others' "weaknesses." Some experts see burnout victims as having difficulty controlling their underlying anger, frustration, and hostility—similar to descriptions of the Type-A personality (see Workshop 4).

Planning to Prevent Burnout

If we know *where* people burn out (workplace situations), *who* burns out (personal characteristics), and *when* people burn out (three-stage process), we should be able to develop a plan to prevent burnout. Early intervention is crucial in preventing job burnout. Some experts believe that prevention needs to start as soon as a person enters a high-stress occupation. The following paragraphs describe some things you can do to prevent burnout:

Workplace Stress

- Learn as much as you possibly can about your chosen career before you begin. Try to find people who are already in the field and talk with them about their experiences. Ask them what they would do differently if they were starting out today. Ask them what they think about the danger of burnout in their field. Ask about the rate of staff turnover; if it is possible to do so, talk to persons who have left the field.
- When your self-worth is low, even minor setbacks and snafus become major crises. You are sensitive to the slightest criticism and don't trust your own judgment. In developing a burnout-prevention plan, avoid situations in which your self-worth is vulnerable to criticism. Value yourself by not trying to live up to others' standards.
- Develop a solid system of values. Set reasonable expectations for yourself. Set your priorities in life and stop worrying about the small stuff.
- Recognize your personal limits. Don't accept responsibility for everything that goes wrong. You can't be responsible for other people's successes or failures (including those of your children!). Stop trying to make the whole world perfect.
- Become aware of your own psychological needs to be liked and approved of by others. Your need for approval may cause you to feel angry with yourself for always "going along." You may also feel angry at yourself for not standing up for what you want to do. Although you may think you are doing a good job of holding your anger in, your irritation might be expressed in a sneaky anger game. If approval is an important reason for working and your chosen field provides little opportunity for obtaining approval, choose another profession.
- Channel your ambition and competitiveness. A strong drive to succeed can help you get through school, break into your professional field, and land you a position with prestige and power. It can also cause problems. If your goals in life are unclear, you may end up striving toward ends that ultimately mean little to you. Or you may turn into a perfectionist and drive everyone around you crazy.

See the "How to Keep from Burning Out" handout for more ideas on this subject.

What Organizations Can Do

Distribute copies of the "Managing to Prevent Burnout" handout to participants and ask them to follow along. Encourage them to offer their own ideas for preventing burnout in the workplace.

Some organizations do little to prevent burnout because they don't appreciate the value of their experienced workers. They may think that it is more cost effective to replace a long-term employee with someone who is willing to take entry-level pay. These organizations fail to realize, however, that experience is valuable and that organizations that keep turning over personnel are inefficient and wasteful.

A job-burnout-prevention plan requires sincere commitment on the part of management. The following paragraphs describe elements that should be considered when developing such a plan.

- Develop a written, comprehensive plan. The plan needs to be endorsed and supported by top management. Appropriate employees should have a copy.
- Offer ongoing support to everyone who is in danger of burning out. Encourage staff to back one another up, to give one another respite from tough work assignments, and to share knowledge and resources.
- Develop procedures for dealing with burnout cases so that people know what to do if they begin to experience the emotional exhaustion that signals the start of burnout.
- When orienting and training new staff members, talk with them about burnout and help them learn about stress management, time management, and distinguishing between excellence (which is possible) and perfection (which is not).
- Teach new employees to set priorities when working under high stress; the importance of time away from work (breaks, rest, and self-care); to be aware of their own motivations, personality, needs, and styles of coping; the dangers of becoming overcommitted and overscheduled.
- Alert employees' family members to the symptoms of job stress and burnout.

The workplace itself can be changed to make it more amenable to the prevention of burnout.

- Vary tasks so that workers aren't doing the same thing every day.
- Limit work hours. Discourage overtime (overtime pay is expensive and people aren't terribly efficient after eight hours, anyway). Offer employees flex-time hours.
- Arrange to have some workers "on call" to pick up the slack when the staff is overloaded.
- Help people focus on what they are doing in the organization by developing a mission statement, precise job descriptions, and maintaining ongoing supervision and training.
- Make the workplace as comfortable and as pleasant as possible so that people look forward to coming to work.
- Be open with regard to concerns about funding and budgeting in order to put an end to rumors and to lower anxiety.
- Streamline paperwork. Trust workers to behave like adults.

- Provide new staff with graduated levels of responsibility.
- Give positive messages to workers. Publicly recognize a tough job that has been done well.

References

1. Christina Maslach, *Burnout: The Cost of Caring* (Englewood Cliffs, NJ: Prentice-Hall, 1982).
2. Martha Bramhall and Susan Ezell, "Working Your Way Out of Burnout," *Public Welfare* 39 (Spring 1981), pp. 32–39.
3. Herbert J. Freudenberger, with Geraldine Richelson, *Burnout: The High Cost of High Achievement* (Garden City, NY: Anchor Press, 1980).
4. Maslach, *Burnout: The Cost of Caring*, p. 65

Handout

Outline for Workshop 8

I. Introduction
II. Overcoming Burnout
   A. Identify stressors
   B. Set realistic goals
   C. Try doing things differently
   D. Take breaks
   E. Leave work at work
   F. Don't overidentify with the workplace
   G. Develop a support system with co-workers
III. Developing a Plan to Overcome Burnout
   A. Enlist your supervisor's support
   B. Cut back on work tasks that are emotionally draining
   C. Rest
   D. Exercise
   E. Develop outlets for your feelings
   F. Eat sensibly and well
   G. Learn to say "no"
   H. Ask for help
   I. Explore other career options
IV. Preventing Burnout
   A. Determine whether you are at risk of burnout
   B. Develop plans to prevent burnout
   C. What organizations can do to prevent burnout
      1. Commitment of management
      2. Changes in the workplace

Workplace Stress

Handout

How to Keep from Burning Out

- Master the skills of stress management, time management, and self-care. Resolve to take care of yourself.
- Know yourself well enough to understand your needs, your ideals, and how you react to stress.
- Restore balance to your life—save time and energy for your family, friends, hobbies, and recreational pursuits.
- Give up on perfectionism. Learn to let some things go.
- Develop a realistic plan for your career.
- Participate in activities with others in your field, especially those that permit people to "let their hair down" and share real concerns.
- Keep growing as a professional, even after you complete your formal education, by reading, going to workshops, and talking to others in similar positions.
- Avoid getting into a rut. Review your career path every 18 months and make changes, if it appears necessary to do so. Remember that even if you can't move up, you may still be able to move laterally.
- Stay tuned in to the danger signals of burnout!

Adapted with permission from Martha Bramhall and Susan Ezell, "How Agencies Can Prevent Burnout," *Public Welfare* 39 (Spring 1981), p. 36.

Handout

Managing to Prevent Burnout

People are not "disposable work units"; they are a valuable resource deserving of respect and consideration. Supervisors can save their company the cost and trouble of having to replace these resources by initiating plans to prevent burnout in the workplace.

➤ *Develop a comprehensive plan:*

If you try to do this piecemeal, the result may be that nobody will understand the plan. Put your plan in writing, get it signed by top management (to indicate that it has their blessing and that they are committed to it), and make sure everyone affected has a copy.

➤ *Offer ongoing support to employees who are in danger of burning out:*

Encourage staff to back each other up, to give each other respite from the toughest problems, and to share knowledge and resources.

➤ *Develop procedures for dealing with burnout:*

Let people know what to do when they start feeling the emotional exhaustion that signals potential burnout.

➤ *Talk to new employees about burnout during orientation and training:*

Help them learn about stress management, time management, and distinguishing between excellence (possible) and perfectionism (not possible).

➤ *Help new employees understand the following:*

How to set priorities when working under high stress; the importance of time away from work—taking breaks, resting, and self-care; the effect of one's motivations, personality, needs, and styles of coping; the dangers of becoming overcommitted and overscheduled.

➤ *Alert employees' family members to the symptoms of job stress and burnout.*

Ways to Diminish Burnout in the Workplace[1]

- Vary tasks so workers don't have the same schedule every day.

- Limit work hours. Discourage overtime (overtime pay is expensive and people aren't terribly efficient after eight hours, anyway) and offer employees flex-time.

- Arrange to have some workers "on call" to pick up the slack when the staff becomes overloaded with work.

- Help people focus on what they are doing in the organization—develop a mission statement, accurate job descriptions, and maintain ongoing supervision and training.

- Make the workplace as comfortable and pleasant as possible so that people look forward to coming in every day.

- Bring concerns about funding and budgeting into the open to put an end to rumors and to lower anxiety.

- Streamline paperwork—trust workers to behave like adults.

- Provide staff with carefully graduated and increased levels of responsibility.

- Give positive messages to workers—publicly recognize a tough job done well.

1. Adapted with permission from Martha Bramhall and Susan Ezell, "Working Your Way Out of Burnout," *Public Welfare* 39 (Spring 1981), pp. 32–39.

Workshop 8

Handout

To Whom It May Concern

Burnout is signaled by emotional exhaustion, depersonalization, and a reduced sense of personal accomplishment. It's a response to the chronic emotional stress caused by dealing with other people, particularly people who are having serious social or psychological problems. This handout can help you explain to the people with whom you work what you are going through. It may help you get their support and cooperation to overcome burnout.

I believe that I may be suffering from the syndrome called "job burnout," because I have been able to identify the following symptoms:

Emotional exhaustion
[ ] I'm experiencing job stress, mostly from dealing with people.
[ ] I feel drained, used up, lack energy.
[ ] I often feel that I am very close to my limits.

Depersonalization
[ ] I don't view the people whom I work with as "real people" any more.
[ ] I can't bring myself to care about their problems.
[ ] I feel I've lost my touch (this distresses me, but I can't help it).
[ ] I feel guilty because I can't care any more.
[ ] I feel like a failure—nothing I do seems to help matters.

Reduced sense of personal accomplishment
[ ] I'm not really doing much—just hanging in there.
[ ] I feel worthless and useless.
[ ] I feel angry for failing, helpless to fix myself, depressed.

Other signs that indicate I am burning out on the job:
_____
_____
_____
_____

Workplace Stress

Handout

Evaluation Form

Job burnout is a condition in which victims change from competent, enthusiastic problem solvers into uninterested, unmotivated pencil pushers, unable and unwilling to expend more than the minimum amount of time or energy on the job. In this workshop we discussed how to overcome burnout and how you can develop a plan to prevent burnout.

Learning Objectives:
- To explore the different choices a burnout victim can make.
- To learn how to develop a plan for recovering from burnout.
- To understand the changes that can be made to prevent future job burnout.

Please respond to these questions by circling the answer with which you agree. Your comments will be used to improve future programs.

1. The presenter fulfilled my expectations of what I wanted to learn from this workshop.

    Very much   Pretty much   Somewhat   Not at all

    Comments: _____
    _____
    _____

2. I can use the information I obtained in this workshop in my job and/or personal relations.

    Very much   Pretty much   Somewhat   Not at all

    Comments: _____
    _____
    _____

3. The presenter knew the material, was organized, and presented the information clearly.

   Very much   Pretty much   Somewhat   Not at all

   Comments: _____
   _____
   _____
   _____

4. What would you have liked the presenter to do differently?
   _____
   _____
   _____
   _____

5. What did you like most about this workshop?
   _____
   _____
   _____
   _____

Workshop 9

➤ Competition and Cooperation

Learning Objectives
- ➤ To investigate popular beliefs about competition and determine whether these beliefs are supported by scientific research.
- ➤ To compare competition with other problem-solving methods.
- ➤ To examine how our attitudes toward winning and losing increase the anxiety, stress, frustration, and anger in our lives.

Introduction

Competition and competitiveness are so deeply ingrained in modern American culture that we rarely question why we are such a competitive people. The subject matter of this workshop may be considered controversial by some, but scientific research backs up each point that is made.

Not all competitive situations are bad, nor are all cooperative ones good. In this workshop, we will analyze competition and competitiveness—what they are and are not, whether alternatives are available.

Recent economic slumps have made businesses reexamine the nature of competition and competitiveness in the workplace. American business organizations have increasingly adopted a collaborative approach. For example, Ford, Chrysler, and General Motors have agreed to work together to produce an electric car. Another important development has been a change from the "vertical structure" of traditional business organizations to a horizontal structure that emphasizes teamwork and cooperation. Educators, too, are concerned about the effects of a competitive environment on their students. Many have gotten away from grading on a "curve" and now encourage students to work collaboratively in learning and problem solving.

Workplace Stress

Interactive discussions are important to the success of this workshop. Competitiveness is so much a part of our culture that many people are reluctant to share their negative feelings about it. The instructor should encourage participants to weigh the advantages and disadvantages of competition for themselves on the basis of their own experiences and to be as objective as possible. If time permits, the instructor may wish to divide the workshop into small groups and have each group focus on a different set of questions. Discussion questions about competitiveness are located at the end of the workshop.

Handouts

- Workshop Outline
- Comparison of Approaches to Problem Solving
- Fun without Competition
- Bibliography
- Evaluation Form

The Trouble with Competitiveness

Make a list of what you like about competition. For example,
- I like the thrill of beating my opponent—winning is exhilarating!
- I like knowing that I can do something better than anyone else.
- Competition keeps me on my toes.
- Competition helps resolve disputes over who's the best.
- Competition challenges me to grow and become a better person.

There are various approaches to life: you can compete with others, you can cooperate with others, or you can act independently. Look at your list of what you like about competition. Is competition the best way to handle life situations? Might another approach work better in some situations?

Americans are taught to compete at an early age. Competition is part of our cultural heritage; we gravitate toward races and contests that match one individual or team against another. This workshop challenges popular beliefs about the merits of competition. But to challenge such beliefs is to invite strong reactions. You may be told that the reason you don't like competition is "because you are afraid of it." People may confuse noncompetitiveness with issues of personal conflict, poor achievement, or survival.

In fact, our notions of competition are often based on misconceptions about its benefits and usefulness.[1] For example,
- Competition is an unavoidable part of human nature—a fact of human life.
- Competition makes us productive and motivates us to do our best.
- Competitive games and sports are good entertainment. The "thrill of victory" satisfies our recreational needs.

> Competition builds character and self-confidence. It teaches us important lessons about winning and losing.

None of these four assumptions is supported by scientific research or modern social psychology. They deserve a closer look.

Is Competition Part of Human Nature?

Is competition inevitable in humans? Is it part of human nature or is it something we learn?

One school of thought holds that just about everything we do is a form of competition and that people who don't appear to be competitive have simply found ways to conceal their competitiveness. Other experts, whose position is supported by scientific evidence, contend that cooperation is more natural than competitiveness and argue that society's existence depends on cooperation.

Most of us have learned to view the world as a jungle where "survival of the fittest" and "dog-eat-dog" are rules that we must live by.[2] Competition is much more dramatic and exciting than cooperation and has become the dominant image portrayed by the media. Biologists are raised in a competitive culture and thus tend to perceive competitive behaviors in other species. In addition, natural selection, the term used to describe the evolutionary process, has been misinterpreted to describe a competitive (and imaginary) struggle for survival. To biologists, natural selection is the process by which nature favors species that are able to adapt to their environment better than other species. Nonscientists often confuse natural selection with dominance and aggressive mating behaviors. Adaptation, however, means fitting into one's ecological niche—being more skillful at gathering food, maintaining a balanced position along the food chain, taking care of one's young, and finding nonfatal ways of resolving conflicts with other members of the same species.[3]

Any example of a successful noncompetitive society or individual should be enough to refute the argument that competition is part of human nature, but people seem to need more evidence to be convinced. We assume that competition is innate because we are accustomed to it. However, scientific evidence indicates that people can be cooperative and succeed.[4] Competitiveness is a learned behavior.

How Do We Learn to Be Competitive?

If we are not competitive by nature, how and when do we learn to be competitive? Children receive messages about competition at an early age—the importance of being the fastest, the biggest, the strongest, the smartest. Some families teach their children that winning is everything and competition is inevitable. Children from these families may learn to compete for their parents' love. In such families, competition between siblings may even be encouraged.

Competing to win is as American as is apple pie. In American culture, we make sports personalities our heroes and often ignore those who have made significant achievements in the sciences, literature, and the arts. The competitive and aggressive lawyer and businessperson are admired and emulated.

We also learn about competition in school, where many teachers introduce it as a social norm. Although some educators might protest that they stress cooperation in the classroom, too often teachers define cooperation as compliance and the ability to follow directions. Evidence from studies of other cultures demonstrates that the United States is unique in its attitude toward competition.[5]

Generally speaking, American children are not taught to value cooperation as an alternative to competition, although in the past few decades American educators have begun to consider research studies that show that it is possible to teach children cooperation, that children do retain what they've learned about cooperation, and that later in life they prefer cooperation over competition.[6]

Adults often compare themselves with others to evaluate abilities and success. Children use social comparisons to form their individual identities. Because social comparisons are inevitable, some experts argue that competition is also inevitable.[7] But it's possible to compare oneself with others without deciding who is "better," which is exactly what well-adjusted adults are able to do.

The important issue here is the significance that one attaches to these comparisons. One's degree of competitiveness depends on how frequently and how strongly the person feels a need to see him- or herself as "better" than others. Competition is not an inevitable part of human nature. It is part of a learned value system supported by our culture. For example,

- Our legal system follows an adversarial model. Each side presents its case to an impartial judge who enforces the rules of fairness and decides who wins and who loses. In other areas of the world, people often resolve disputes with the help of a mediator—the opposing sides try to work out their own solution through an objective third party.
- Sports and games, in which the emphasis is on scoring and winning.
- Teachers who grade on a curve, forcing students to compete for a limited number of high grades.
- Hiring and promotion.
- Admission to schools and colleges.

- Bidding on contracts—vendors compete on price, speed, and quality.
- Artists' competitions in the fields of dance, music, visual arts, and literature.
- Beauty contests.
- Political campaigns.

Does Competition Make People More Productive?

Another erroneous popular belief equates competition with productivity. It is argued that competition brings out the best in people. Productivity has been an especially important issue in recent years as economic and political forces have made us focus on the productivity of the American work force. If we don't maintain a high level of productivity, the argument states, we won't be able to compete in world markets.

But we must ask ourselves whether we perform better when we try to beat others, when we work cooperatively with others, or when we work alone. Review the "Comparison of Approaches to Problem Solving" handout and try to think of problems that might be easier to resolve by means of a cooperative approach.

Ask workshop participants for their perspectives on competition versus cooperation or working alone. Ask them whether they perform better when they try to beat others, when they work with others (cooperation), or when they work alone (individual effort). Participants can use the handout to compare the advantages and disadvantages of each approach applied to the examples offered.

How does competition measure up against cooperation and individual effort? An analysis of 122 research studies done between 1924 and 1980 found that people almost never work better in a competitive situation.[8] People working in cooperative groups performed better, regardless of whether their group was working independently or competing with other groups.

What Are You Competing For?

People usually expect a reward for winning. Depending on the reward, people are expected to be more or less competitive. However, although researchers have found that "winner take all" reward systems may result in an increase in speed, the quality of performance is diminished.[9]

People perform best in tasks that they enjoy. Thus, extrinsic motivators such as money or points are never as psychologically satisfying as performing a task that is enjoyable and rewarding in itself.

When emphasis is placed on external motivators, internal motivation is weakened and people no longer do things because they enjoy them. Job-burnout victims are workers who have lost sight of the intrinsic rewards of a job well done and thus no longer find their work interesting, challenging, fun, or valuable. Often, they work only for the money.

Why doesn't competition result in superior performance? The answer lies in the fact that trying to beat others is very different from trying to perform well. When you compete with others, you have less energy available to make your product good. In competitive situations, synergy—the energy that comes from having a group of people tackle a problem together—is lacking. Competitors aren't able to use all of the resources that might be available if they worked cooperatively. Moreover, competition tends to discourage openness and sharing as well as to make people hostile and secretive.

Competition and Anxiety

Competition inhibits productivity because it is stressful and produces anxiety. True, a degree of stress can increase productivity. However, for every task an optimum level of arousal exists—the more complex a task is, the lower is its corresponding optimum level of arousal.[10]

Part of the anxiety caused by competition comes from thinking that you may lose. The shame and humiliation of being publicly defeated increase stress and anxiety. Anxiety may also result from winning—the guilt from causing other people to lose, the fear of making enemies, the concern that others will resent you for winning. Finally, competitors often dehumanize their opponents, perceiving them as obstacles to winning. Rather than making people want to win, anxiety makes many people desperate to avoid failure. In such cases, people may go out of their way to avoid competitive situations and feel miserable doing so.

Competitive Recreational Activities

Many adults believe that competitive sports and games are the most appropriate and enjoyable kinds of play. But how do we define play? Is play the same thing as competition or is it different?

Ask workshop participants for their definitions of play. Don't be surprised if people define play by the activities in which they engage. Encourage discussion of the following definitions of play. You may wish to display these items on an overhead transparency or flipchart. For an interesting discussion of Americans' attitudes toward play, see Norman Lobsenz, "Do You Really Know How to Play?" Parade Magazine (June 3, 1990), p. 20.

➤ Play is voluntary.
➤ Play is fun and pleasing in itself. Although play can help you master a skill or performance, that is not the reason you play.

➤ Play has no goal other than having fun.
➤ Play often involves trying new things, meeting challenges, and overcoming them.
➤ Play is a more or less spontaneous activity. If it includes too many rules, it's not fun.

If we play to relax, then play should be something that reduces stress. Some people find competitive sports very stressful. The degree of stress people feel depends on how seriously they take sports. Americans' attitudes toward sports indicate that we take athletic competitions very seriously; winning is emphasized and often little consideration is given to fun. When athletes feel such pressure to win, the emphasis shifts from the fun of doing something well to the stress of winning at all costs. This attitude takes the fun and playfulness out of competitive sports. In addition, competitive sports often have lots of rules that can inhibit the sense of play, and players are frequently motivated by extrinsic factors such as money, the desire to gain the approval of others, and prestige and status.

Another problem with competition as recreation is that some people confuse achievement with competition. They insist that keeping score encourages players to do their best. However, many studies indicate that one's goals can be achieved as easily through independent or cooperative activity as they can through competitive activity.[11]

Distribute the "Fun without Competition" handout and ask participants to follow along as you go through the pros and cons of competition as recreation.[12] Use it to stimulate discussion of the attitudes and values involved in sports. Participants who are parents might comment on how they feel about having their children involved in competitive sports.[13] The handout is self-explanatory and need not be read in the workshop.

Pros and Cons of Athletic Competition

Exercise: Playing sports improves a person's strength, endurance, and coordination.	Exercise does not require competition.
Teamwork: Being part of an athletic team teaches you interpersonal skills, promotes camaraderie and group loyalty.	Camaraderie is precisely what makes cooperative activities so rewarding. "Fighting" against a common enemy (us vs. them) is not necessary to establish a group feeling.

Zest: Competition makes recreational activities exciting and interesting.	Leisure activities that calm, rest, and restore energy can be rewarding and enjoyable.
Challenge: Competition allows you to push your personal limits and to excel.	Noncompetitive striving can be very rewarding. Don't confuse achievement with competition.
Strategy: Athletic competitions provide a structured environment in which you can anticipate and counter another player's moves.	Overcoming obstacles and solving interesting problems can be fun, but you don't need competition to test your skills. Noncompetitive activities can also provide pleasure.
Total involvement: Competition may provide an exhilarating experience that transcends day-to-day living.	Competition is not the only type of activity that allows one to feel totally involved and to experience a sense of "existential affirmation." Activities that require creativity, overcoming adversity, and facing new challenges provide similar experiences.
Thrill of victory: Triumphing over others is an intrinsically satisfying experience.	Relishing a victory that comes from beating someone else may be a sign of low self-esteem and can harm your interpersonal relationships.

Of these items, only the last one requires competition. So why do competitive games play such a large role in our culture? The number of adults who actually participate in competitive sports is not really that high. Approximately 80%–90% of children drop out of organized sports by the time they are 15 years old.[14] They drop out for various reasons but many say that they simply don't like competition. Competitive sports also turn off many parents, who become unhappy with schools that emphasize athletics over academics.

Educators who introduce the concept of noncompetitive games to their pupils are witnessing interesting results. When children are offered noncompetitive games, many prefer them over competitive games.

Many people believe that competition is good because it helps build character. Training, psychological and physical preparation, learning new skills, enduring pain and discomfort, working as part of a team, sacrificing oneself for the good of the team are touted as character-building activities of competition.

Critics of competition, however, state that these lessons can also be learned through noncompetitive activities. They say that competition doesn't necessarily build character and point to the negative psychological and interpersonal effects of competition.[15] They argue that one psychological explanation for why people compete is that they need to overcome fundamental doubts about their own abilities and to compensate for low self-esteem.[16]

Some people say that competition teaches important lessons about fairness, playing by the rules, and good sportsmanship. But if fairness must be enforced by squads of referees, umpires, and the hundreds of people who see to it that players, teams, coaches, owners, concession operators, broadcasters, stadium owners, and the rest all play by the rules, we can only conclude that people can't be trusted to play fair on their own. The lesson of sportsmanship is all too often "see what you can get away with." In contrast, character and a solid value system are gained from growing up in an environment in which positive values are nurtured.

Competition in the Workplace

Kohn distinguishes between structural competition and intentional competition. *Structural competition* is situational, wherein we are placed in a win/lose situation by circumstances (e.g., when applying for a job). *Intentional competition* is internal and comes from the individual's need to prove his or her superiority.

American business organizations have traditionally operated within a framework of structural competition—a hierarchical system in which individuals compete for jobs, promotions, and status. New ideas about quality, however, have forced businesses to review the benefits of this approach. Not surprisingly, many business leaders have replaced "management by results" with the quality leadership philosophies of Juran and Deming, who place greater value on teamwork and cooperation than on competition. Quality leadership stresses collaboration with the organization.[17]

The new organizational philosophies also reject internal competition and the constant need to compare one's achievements with others. Business organizations are increasingly interested in recruiting team players with strong interpersonal skills. Employees are finding that they must change their attitudes in order to adapt to this new corporate culture.

Today, one even finds a new spirit of cooperation among rival business organizations. An agreement by the "Big Three" automakers jointly to produce an electric vehicle is just one example of this phenomenon. Collaboration is no longer perceived as a threat to the survival of *laissez-faire* capitalism; rather, it is viewed as necessary for its survival.

Cooperation as an Alternative to Competition

It may be difficult to change from a competitive to a cooperative organizational structure, but it is certainly not impossible to do so. When structural competition is replaced by cooperation, it becomes easier to do away with intentional competition and the resultant stress in the workplace.

Competition is not always the best way to achieve one's goals. Collaborative efforts can be just as productive. Working as part of a team requires good communications skills and the ability to coordinate one's plans with others. Teamwork is a source of synergy, whereby collaborative efforts produce more than individual efforts. Moreover, individuals in conflict are more likely to abide by solutions arrived at through a cooperative conflict-resolution process than by decisions handed down by those who must choose a winner and a loser. Students learn more—about their course work and about interpersonal relations—when they work in teams.

Ask participants to review the "Comparison of Approaches to Problem Solving" handout. Ask them to fill in the advantages and disadvantages of the three primary problem-solving modes. How do these different modes compare with one another?

Conclusion

We have discussed how competition increases anxiety, drives people apart, and prevents people from doing things in the most productive and efficient way. Competition can also cause people to believe that they are not in control of what happens to them; because they don't make the rules, their successes and failures are attributable to others, which helps create a sense of helplessness, frustration, and anger.

Because competition is the accepted norm in our society, when we compete we feel "normal." By doing what is expected of us, we feel better about ourselves. As a result, many people have mixed feelings about competing, winning, and losing.

Studies have shown that self-esteem rises in a cooperative environment. In a competitive environment, one person or team wins and the others lose. Losing can be humiliating and can make people feel inadequate. Losing doesn't add to self-esteem; at best, it may not harm your self-image. And winning can't compensate for losing, because victory is never permanent. A winner immediately becomes the target of his or her rivals. Competition breeds more competition.

People who are highly competitive sometimes have trouble understanding the concepts presented in this workshop. They have always competed and can't see why it is a problem. It may be very difficult for them to accept the fact that many people are turned off by competition. Similarly, those who consistently avoid competition may need to learn to appreciate some people's need to compete. The goal of this workshop is to create a dialogue between these two points of view.

We have by no means exhausted the subject of competition in culture and society. If time permits, the instructor may wish to ask participants the following questions. Or the instructor may wish to have a group of participants discuss these questions in a panel format; include participants with different points of view on the panel.

➤ Losing isn't equivalent to personal failure. Why do some people take winning so seriously? Why do we get such mixed messages about winning and losing: for example, "losing doesn't matter," but "nice guys finish last."

➤ It's important for society to have rules, and competition is one of the best ways to teach children to follow the rules. What happens when no penalties are incurred for breaking the rules? What happens when the rules are not enforced, enforced sporadically, or used to discriminate? Do too many rules merely encourage people to try to find ways to get around them?

➤ Our legal system is adversarial. Each side presents its case to an impartial judge who enforces the rules of fairness and decides who wins and who loses. In other countries, disputes may be resolved with the help of a mediator or ombudsman. Does competition lead to rigid, either/or thinking and cause people to frame problems in terms of good vs. evil, them vs. us? Is an adversarial procedure the best system for handling family disputes, divorces, and custody battles? What would happen if the judge didn't have to pick a winner and a loser but could rule that both sides deserved to win a little? Is there any advantage to having the different sides try to work out their own solution?

➤ Americans have been accused of being greedy and materialistic. We are always trying to buy more, own more, experience more. Does competition foster the notion that owning things is the most important symbol of success?

➤ Some people say that so many rules govern manufacturing, employment, marketing, and tax laws that we don't really have a competitive

marketplace. Is our "free market" economic system really competitive?
- Competition can only work if everyone agrees on the rules and goes after the same goals. Is conformity one result of competition? Does competition have a dampening effect on creativity?
- Competition is not always the best way to achieve one's goals. In some situations might approaches other than competition be more appropriate?

Consider the following examples. Ask participants whether competition is the best or only approach that could be used in each situation:

Courses for which the teacher grades on the curve
Hiring the best person for a job
Being considered for a promotion
When selling something
In court, on either side of a lawsuit
Sports and games
Artistic competitions (dance, music, visual arts, poetry, or literature)
Beauty contests
When supporting a political candidate (or running for office yourself)

- When resources are scarce, competition is the only rational response. What else can you do when only one job, one portion of food, or one of any other desirable thing is available? What happens when you consider the causes of the shortage, the consequences of competing for resources, and the context in which the competition occurs?
- Accountability to others—not money or victory—is a powerful human motivator. And accountability requires cooperation. Americans take an individualistic perspective and say, "What's in it for me?" whereas Asians consider what's best for the group. How do the American and Asian perspectives differ? What are the benefits of cooperation? Should our actions, behaviors, and organizational goals reflect greater concern for the welfare of the group?

References

1. Alfie Kohn, *No Contest: The Case against Competition* (Boston: Houghton Mifflin, 1986), p. 6.
2. Ibid., p. 22.
3. George Gaylord Simpson, *The Meaning of Evolution* (New Haven, CT: Yale University Press, 1949), p. 222.
4. Kohn, *No Contest*.
5. Ibid., p. 2.
6. Ibid., p. 32; Terry Orlick, *Winning through Cooperation: Competitive Insanity,*

Cooperative Alternatives (Washington, DC: Acropolis Books, 1978), p. 177.

7. Kohn, *No Contest*, p. 41.
8. David W. Johnson, Geoffrey Maruyama, Roger Johnson, Deborah Nelson, and Linda Skon, "Effects of Cooperative, Competitive, and Individualistic Goal Structures on Achievement: A Meta-Analysis," *Psychological Bulletin* 89 (1981), pp. 45–62. When competition was compared with cooperation, in 65 cases cooperative efforts fared better than competitive activities, in 36 cases no statistically significant difference was found between the two, and in 8 cases competition worked better than cooperation. The same studies showed that when cooperation was compared with individual effort, cooperation worked better in 108 cases, individual effort worked better in 6 cases, and no significant difference was found in 42 cases. These studies offer some tentative conclusions: Cooperation works better when the group is small and the task is more complex; competition works better when the task is simple and not interdependent.
9. Kohn, *No Contest*, p. 49.
10. Ibid., p. 63.
11. Ibid., p. 49.
12. Ibid., p. 91.
13. For more information on how competition affects children, see Benjamin Spock, "No Contest (Competition and Children)," *Parenting* 7 (March 1993), p. 110, and Julius Segal and Zelda Segal, "Competition (As They Grow: 5 and 6), *Parenting Magazine* 67 (March 1992), p. 161.
14. Terry Orlick, *Winning through Cooperation: Competitive Insanity, Cooperative Alternatives* (Washington, DC: Acropolis Books, 1978), p. 92.
15. Despite all the talk about how competition builds character, studies indicate that athletic competition actually inhibits personal growth, that athletes suffer from high levels of stress and depression, and that they tend to have relatively shallow relationships with others. Strength of character does not require competition. In fact, many people with considerable strength of character avoid competitive activities. Researchers have found that athletes don't develop more character strengths through competition; whatever strengths they have, they had before they began competing. See Bruce C. Ogilvie and Thomas A. Tutko, "Sport: If You Want to Build Character, Try Something Else," *Psychology Today* 5 (October 1971), pp. 61–63.
16. A person's behavior is said to be "deficit motivated" when he or she does things to compensate for something he or she lacks. When people lack self-esteem, their need to compete may become urgent. Without competition, they literally have no self-identity. For these people, lack of competition can be a terrible prospect. Competition fulfills their need for approval from others. Competitive people are never satisfied just knowing they can do something; they must prove it over and over. See Kohn, *No Contest*, p. 99.
17. Peter R. Scholtes, *The Team Handbook: How to Use Teams to Improve Quality* (Madison, WI: Joiner Associates, 1988), pp. 1–8.

Workplace Stress

Handout

Outline for Workshop 9

 I. Introduction
 II. The Trouble with Competitiveness
    A. Competing, cooperating, acting independently
    B. Misconceptions about the benefits of competition
 III. Is Competition Part of Human Nature?
    A. Is competitiveness innate or learned?
    B. Natural selection
    C. Competitiveness is a learned behavior
 IV. How Do We Learn to Be Competitive?
    A. Children receive messages about competition
    B. American culture
    C. Competition in school
    D. Comparing oneself with others
 V. Does Competition Make People More Productive?
    A. Performance as it relates to competition versus cooperation
    B. "Comparison of Approaches to Problem Solving" handout
 VI. What Are You Competing For?
    A. Reward systems
    B. Intrinsic versus extrinsic rewards
 VII. Competition and Anxiety
 VIII. Competitive Recreational Activities
    A. Sports and games
    B. Playing to relax
    C. Confusing achievement with competition
    D. Pros and cons of athletic competition
 IX. Competition in the Workplace
    A. Structural competition versus intentional competition
    B. New organizational philosophies
 X. Cooperation as an Alternative to Competition
 XI. Conclusion
    A. Mixed feelings about competing, winning, and losing
    B. Self-esteem
    C. Societal messages about competition and cooperation

Handout

Comparison of Approaches to Problem Solving

Compare three different approaches to solving problems. *Cooperation* involves several people working together to find a solution. In *competition*, people or groups work separately and against each other. In *individual* effort, one person works alone, without regard for others. List the advantages and disadvantages of each approach in the matrix below.

Method	Advantages	Disadvantages
Cooperation	_____	_____
	_____	_____
	_____	_____
Competition	_____	_____
	_____	_____
	_____	_____
Individual effort	_____	_____
	_____	_____
	_____	_____

Do we perform better when trying to beat others, when working with them, or working alone? Johnson and co-workers' analysis of 122 research studies conducted between 1924 and 1980 found that in 65 cases cooperative work was better than competition, in 36 cases no statistically significant difference was found between the two, and in 8 cases competition worked better than cooperation.

The same study found that cooperation worked better than individual work in 108 cases, individual effort worked better in 6 cases, and no significant difference was found in 42 cases. Thus a cooperative approach to problem-solving seems to have definite advantages.

These studies drew the following conclusions: Cooperation works better when the group is small and the task is more complex; competition works when the task is simple and competitors don't have to rely on one another for anything.[1]

1. David W. Johnson, Geoffrey Maruyama, Roger Johnson, Deborah Nelson, and Linda Skon, "Effects of Cooperative, Competitive, and Individualistic Goal Structures on Achievement: A Meta-Analysis," *Psychological Bulletin* 89 (1981), pp. 45–62.

Workplace Stress

Handout

Fun without Competition

Athletic competitions are extremely popular, even though some say they don't really qualify as "play." People who enjoy these activities often give the following arguments for why they enjoy competitive sports.

Reason	Response
Exercise: Playing sports improves a person's strength, endurance, and coordination.	Exercise does not require competition.
Teamwork: Being part of an athletic team teaches you interpersonal skills, promotes camaraderie and group loyalty.	Camaraderie is precisely what makes cooperative activities so rewarding. "Fighting" against a common enemy (us vs. them) isn't necessary to establish a group feeling.
Zest: Competition makes recreational activities exciting and interesting.	Leisure activites that calm, rest, and restore energy can be enjoyable and rewarding.
Challenge: Competition allows you to push your personal limits and to excel.	Noncompetitive striving can be very rewarding; don't confuse achievement with competition.
Strategy: Athletic competitions provide a structured environment in which you can anticipate and counter another player's moves.	Overcoming obstacles and solving interesting problems can be fun, but you don't need competition to test your skills. Noncompetitive activities can also provide pleasure.

Total involvement: Competition may provide you with an exhilarating experience that transcends day-to-day living.

Competition is not the only type of activity that allows one to become totally involved and experience "existential affirmation." Activities that require a sense of creativity, overcoming adversity, and facing new challenges provide similar experiences.

Thrill of victory: Triumphing over others is an intrinsically satisfying experience.

Relishing a victory that comes from beating someone else may be a sign of low self-esteem and can harm your interpersonal relationships.

Adapted with permission from Alfie Kohn, *No Contest: The Case against Competition* (Boston: Houghton Mifflin, 1986), p. 91.

Handout

Bibliography

Gaylin, Willard (1984). *The Rage Within: Anger in Modern Life.* New York: Simon and Schuster.

Johnson, David W., & Roger T. Johnson (1975). *Learning Together and Alone: Cooperation, Competition, and Individualization.* Englewood Cliffs, NJ: Prentice-Hall.

Kohn, Alfie (1986). *No Contest: The Case against Competition.* Boston: Houghton Mifflin.

Lappe, Frances Moore (1989). *Rediscovering America's Values.* New York: Ballantine Books.

Lasch, Christopher (1979). *The Culture of Narcissism: American Life in an Age of Diminishing Expectations.* New York: Warner Communications.

Ruben, Harvey L. (1981). *Competing.* New York: Pinnacle Books.

Walker, Stuart H. (1980). *Winning: The Psychology of Competition.* New York: W. W. Norton.

Handout

Evaluation Form

Competition and competitiveness have become so deeply a part of modern American culture that we rarely stop and question how and why they become part of our lives. In this workshop, we looked at what these behaviors are, what they are not, and considered the advantages of alternatives to competition.

Learning Objectives:
- To understand that many popular beliefs about competition are not supported by scientific research.
- To learn how to compare competition with other methods of problem solving.
- To examine whether our attitudes toward winning and losing increase the anxiety, stress, frustration, and anger in our lives.

Please respond to these questions by circling the answers you agree with. Your comments will be used to help improve future programs.

1. The presenter fulfilled my expectations of what I wanted to learn from this workshop.

    Very much   Pretty much   Somewhat   Not at all

    Comments: _____
    _____
    _____
    _____

2. I can use the information I obtained in this workshop in my job and/or personal relations.

    Very much   Pretty much   Somewhat   Not at all

    Comments: _____
    _____
    _____
    _____

Workplace Stress

3. The presenter knew the material, was organized, and presented the information clearly.

   Very much   Pretty much   Somewhat   Not at all

   Comments: _____
   _____
   _____
   _____

4. What would you have liked the presenter to do differently?
   _____
   _____
   _____
   _____

5. What did you like most about this workshop?
   _____
   _____
   _____
   _____